WHORL BOOKS • HAUNTED BY HISTORY SERIES

Did a serial killer stalk early day Oklahoma?

WHEN DEATH RODE THE RAILS:
Some strange deaths along Oklahoma Rails, 1900-1920

By

Marilyn A. Hudson

Copyright 2011, Marilyn A. Hudson

>   Whorl Books
>   5658 NW Pioneer Circle
>   Norman, Oklahoma 73072

Note: Images may not reflect Oklahoma sites. Some are used for illustrative purposes only.

Hudson, Marilyn A.
When death rode the rails: some strange deaths along Oklahoma railroads, 1900 to 1920. Norman, Oklahoma: Whorl Books, 2009.

A reprint of a smaller monograph of 2008.
Description: Strange deaths along early Oklahoma rail lines.

1. Oklahoma – History - Miscellanea. 2. Railroads – Oklahoma. 3. Oklahoma – Crime – History-Misc.

F 697
976.6
H88

Reprinted in partnership with CreateSpace.

FOREWARD

As a child I dreaded being in the first automobile waiting at the railroad crossing.

The long freight and passenger trains slowed down in town. They still, however, seemed capable of sucking the unwary right under those huge, and perpetually rusty, metal wheels shooting sparks as they passed. I would shrink back into the passenger seat, my foot pressing down on an invisible brake, and eyes closed in a fervent prayer that the monster would pass by one more time.

Walking a field once with friends, warned against going down along the tracks, I watched an old workhorse engine pull ancient cars to a roundhouse for retirement. The ground shook at the monster's passing, the noise made us shout, and the rush of air pushed ahead of the engine was a palatable thing with a devilish personality. It could inspire the wide-eyed and tempt the unwary: optical illusions made it seem a sluggish creature, but it was fast compared to a pedestrian.

Those memories re-emerged and attracted me to stories found in passing as I conducted some historical research and led me to seek out still others. Along the way, questions began to haunt me about how such a monster could ever, even if they were asleep, sneak up on a person? Then, other questions led me to see, what appeared to be, some strange similarities in deaths spread over vast areas.

Regardless of how anyone decides concerning the nature or relationship of these causalities, they are an adventure in the journey. Along the rail way fascinating glimpses of another time are revealed. The challenges they faced provided insight into how little people really change. Along the way, in every stop, were introduced heroes, scoundrels, and ordinary folk just trying to survive what life had brought their way.

I hope you enjoy this small journey along some strange roads and, like me, find yourself happily haunted by history.

Enjoy,
Marilyn A. Hudson
Norman, Oklahoma
2011

DEDICATIONS

The author dedicates this monograph to her father and step-grandfather who worked the rails as 'gandy men." Roy Terry and Dan V. Willard knew firsthand how difficult the lines could be as they worked tracks in Kansas, Missouri, and Nebraska. They battled extreme winters with snowdrifts as tall as the engines and summer heat and humidity providing the true tales of horror.

She also wishes to thank her sons, Cullan and Jeremy and her husband for their ongoing, tolerant, and usually serious, support. She also wishes to dedicate this work to Dennis, Gary, and Helen.

Finally, she dedicates this to those who work, often without notice or recompense, in communities across the country keeping alive the memory and the potential of the rails. If you are lucky enough to have a historic depot, railroad museum, or a working railroad near you, discover it, celebrate it and support it.

Maybe someday the trains will return in force crisscrossing the land, connecting places with ease and comfort, decongesting roadways and returning just a taste of the most romantic elements of the past. In doing so creating whole new generations who thrill to hear the call of the whistle and the excitement at the wind as the train hurries past.

When Death Rode the Rails

ONCE UPON A TIME......ON THE RIVER OF STEEL

As the rail car slowed down after making the curve outside of town, J.R. Duggan swung smoothly down from the rear. Twilight was settling and the cook fires were already springing up across where the rail crew, those here-today-gone-tomorrow types, and a few rootless families, waited for the next pitiable scrap of a job. When there were no jobs, they just packed and moved on down the lines looking for something better.

It was 1906, and the railroads were still stitching their seams across this soon-to-be new state of Oklahoma. A crazy pattern would make any quilting woman proud. Those down on their luck, or those inclined to do as little as possible, followed the rails and these little camps cropped up all along the lines. He had timed it just right coming in as the dark was falling and the coffee boiling.

Strolling through the camp, making sure he was visible, he shared a cup of coffee. He passed along all the scraps of news he had picked up, as all travelers were obliged to do, in return for the meager hospitality the fires offered. He told what he knew of the news of terrible floods in China, the rail accidents in the northeastern states, and even the latest reports on President Theodore Roosevelt's health.

Quietly, carefully, he moved around the small camp looking at faces and checking to see if he recognized anyone. All strangers this time and that was a relief. There had been a time or two lately he'd seen a fellow, and knew by the glances the man gave him across the camp fire, or during a crew break, that he was thinking about where he'd seen him before. He had had to deal with that already, and would again if he had to, but preferred when he moved as a stranger.

Finally, he found a shadowed corner just out of the range of the fire, and spread out his bedroll, sighing in contentment as weary muscles stretched out.

Listening as the camp went to sleep he longed for his home, the sound of his children laughing and giggling, and the pleasure to be found in just watching his wife sew by the lamp light. They were all lost to him now. A dream that just teased him in the darkest and loneliest moments when he was weak and feeble from long hours of work or long days of his own company.

A sound woke him, the crack of some farmer scaring off a coyote with a shotgun, or perhaps the snap of a rotted branch as a deer passed in the night. He thought one or two others were lying silent and watchful in the night as well. No one moved in the camp, so it was probably his own imagination, and he quickly went back to sleep.

His dreams were not sweet but fevered ones that featured a parade of mangled bodies, gaping holes where throats had been, and blood painting the rails a never-ending red.

As if his dreams had distressed the day, the sky was pewter the next morning when he woke and there was a smell of rain in the air. The air was thick, and the damp undergrowth nearby, brought to mind the sickish aroma of the corrupted flesh of his dreams. Here and there a few women stirred about as they made coffee or tended silent, hungry children. Lanterns coming down the tracks from town indicated the work day was starting.

As the first men came into the camp, however, a silence descended. People began to cluster into small groups and looking fearfully around them. One or two glanced his way as they listened to whatever news the others shared.

Suspicion, honed by years of being right, had Duggan quickly slapping on his shoes and gathering his things together. Over by themselves sat, the two men he had met last night, Clyde and Jacob. The old men, a deep shade of brown and as tough and stringy as dried meat, were once more sitting by a miserable little fire.

"Bad accident happened up the line." He saw the old men glancing over to the newcomers. The man Clyde spat out a knuckle sized wad of tobacco before he dragged his flannel sleeve across his weathered face. He smeared the trailing brown ooze instead of wiping it away. "Feller fell asleep on the tracks and was run over by a train."

"Fell asleep." His companion snorted derisively into the tin can he was using for a cup. "That's a good one right there."

"You men saying he didn't fall asleep?" Duggan hunkered down lowering his voice. He had learned long ago that he could learn a lot in such moments. In his experience, most people were equally curious, as they were willing to gossip. He could learn things that could save his life later.

"Jacob's right. I seen men so falling down drunk they didn't know up from down. I seen men so tuckered out they couldn't move. And once or twice, I seen nights so danged cold, that the warm tracks were a right nice place to stand for a time." He pulled a sagging suspender up over one scrawny shoulder, and then adjusted the other, before he went on. "For a time you understand. Just for a time and then it is gone. You might not be right as rain, but you can leastwise get in out the rain, if you see my drift. Can't say I have ever seen so many people falling asleep on tracks. Seems lately, well it's all the rage."

"That or falling off so many trestles you'd think we had no sense of balance in these parts." His companion added. "Or so mule dumb we just keep been' run down by trains."

Duggan looked over the camp with new eyes as the words sunk in. "There have been quite a few accidents then around here?"

"Plenty of accidents reported all up and down these tracks." Jacob said.

"From Enid down to Noble", Clyde told him, "and from Frederick all the way over to Tulsa."

"Folks in the crews are getting a little cautious now you might say." Jacob told him with a glint in his watery eyes. "So if you don't get the welcome mat down the track, or in one of the towns, don't be surprised. Strangers aren't always welcome right now. The rail folk are playing it close to their chests but it's clear for those who can see."

"A man can't be too careful. So, I know what to look for; tell me about these deaths. What have you heard?"

"Trains are dangerous enough as it is. There was that feller down in the city in '04; he was crushed to death between the cars." Jacob scratched his chin struggling with remembering. "That was awful bad and more than once some man was killed when a hitch failed."

"There are always folks that think they can outrun the train. Perfectly good wagon and horse gone because of some darned fool was too deaf to hear the train coming."

"Those don't seem too strange or extraordinary." Dagon commented with a smile. "What's that saying about 'accidents happen'?"

"That's because they ain't the ones we're talkin' about!" Jacob hissed.

"Now, calm down. He does not know your ways. Jacob has to sort of circle the cabin you understand." Clyde explained making little spirals in the air. "He can't just go right through the front door like a normal person. Can get on the nerves a bit from time to time, yes sir; I will admit."

"Anyways, those are normal hazards, as they say. Since about '03 there's been a lot dead bodies found alongside the tracks all around these parts."

"No goes back to '02." Jacob countered. "October of 1902. That was when those boys died down near Noble. Their folks sued the Santa Fe line."

"Well if you are looking at it that way. They found those bodies down near Frederick and over near the Boggy."

"Yes, Jacob is right. I forgot that. Then there was that farmer, down near Ardmore, struck by a train. Folks said they heard shots. They didn't know if it that one was murder or accident from the start."

"Problem is there's just been too many "accidents" by my reckoning." Clyde stood and helped his friend up, kicking the fire out and shrugging into threadbare denim coats. "There's our ride now. Found us a town job for a while helping fix up a farm. It'll keep us out of the cold for a few months. If I was you son, I'd be doing the same thing." He set off walking toward where a wagon had pulled up with a man and woman of about the same age as the two men.

"These tracks seem to be bad for a man's health." Jacob added before following his friend.

Duggan watched the men, wagon until they were out of sight, and turned to see the camp was now nearly deserted. A small group of men stood by the tracks and from their dress, it was clear they were railroad men waiting for the next train to pick them up. He paused, wondering if he should go on into town or talk with the crew. He turned as he heard a crowd come down the road. A little man led the way with purposeful stride, a thick black cane in one hand, and Duggan knew he had waited too long.

Quicker than he would have thought, the group spread out through the camp. He turned to escape and felt his arms yanked behind his back by a burly farmer, and another shoved a club into his gut. All around him, those remaining in the camp that had not been cornered yet were scattering, charging into the brush on the other side of the tracks, or disappearing down a ravine.

"Killers! I'll get the killers murdered my boy," snarled the small man who had led the group. He roared out into the thick of things spinning like a top, striking out with his wicked looking club. One of the swipes of the club clipped Dugan in the chest; he gasped in sudden pain, and then felt a hard blow to his head. He dropped heavily to his knees.

"Get them all!" The little man was shouting. Working the others into blood frenzy, the little man used his own cane on more than one man.

Even as he felt himself fall to the ground, Dugan tried to get back up and block the next blow, but he was too slow.

"You all are nothing but trash every last man of you. We'll teach you! Get a rope somebody! Hang 'em all!" Face in the rocky dirt, boots pounded his sides as blood erupted from a dozen wounds. "Hang every mother's son of them!"

He heard women screaming and children crying in the distance. Other sounds, much nearer, told him he was not the only one abused. Dragging a couple of men to where one man was uncoiling a rope, several of the newcomers had plans.

Bullets echoed suddenly in the morning air then, and the mob around him halted. Men on horses ran into the camp and Dugan saw the glint of metal on their chests. Shouts and curses followed as a few more shots rang out. Dugan decided to stay where he was in the dirt lest a stray bullet add to his suffering. The sound of men moaning and being violently sick mixed with the snorting of horses and the shouts of the newcomers.

The officers soon had the bitter mob smoothly corralled and, looking down the business end of those rifle barrels, none of them seemed anxious to test the dedication or aim of the newcomers.

Hoisting himself up to his knees he gasped as a deep breath told him a rib was probably broken. Staggering upright, Degan saw that he had been right. Even without the badges on their shirts, each man had a face that was all business. That was especially true of one man without a badge on his dusty black coat.

Black coat edged his dusty sorrel toward where Duggan stood. His thick mustache was more dusted with gray these days. He said: "I should have known you'd be in the thick of things Duggan."

"Bartell." Duggan said, winching at the pain in so simple an action.

Bartell had once been a U.S. Deputy Marshall and then a police officer in Oklahoma City and now ran the Oklahoma Detective Agency. "I take it something else has happened."

"We are not sure yet. Local sheriff wired saying he was afraid things might get a little rough around here so we decided it was a nice day for a ride." He nodded toward the group of men who stood in a tight group.

Their glares toward Duggan, and the newcomers, made a fine steel blade seem dull.

"A young boy about 14 is missing and the general description fits the body they found down the tracks early this morning."

The two men looked at each other and, for years after, all those who witnessed the exchange could never decide whose eyes were colder, or who face was more like death on a mission.

"I am going to get this man. If I have to stay on the trail for years, I will get this man and he will pay the full price." Duggan said at last. He pulled a leather wallet from his pocket and flipped it open to reveal a brass toned badge. He flinched as he set it so that the emblem hung down from his shirt pocket.

The cluster of men watching from behind the ring of guns saw the badge and the two men talking. Their earlier anger began to fade to deep puzzlement and more than a little anxiety.

"You'll need a horse to make the journey." Bartell said as he motioned to one of his men. "Jackson here has a sudden wish to ride the train back to the City and send a message for me. You can take his horse."

Duggan glanced up at Bartell, who was a figure a little bigger than life in the area. He had heard he was a just but tough man, one who did not take guff from anyone and often paid the price. Overall, he was a good man to have around in a tight spot.

"Thank you. You can turn in a requisition to the company for a replacement for your man."

"I'll do that." Bartell smiled from behind his thick mustache. "Do you have any other needs?"

"No." He struggled up into the saddle, tight lipped with pain, but determined to ride. He looked at the corralled men. "Will you be taking care of this lot?"

"We can't have people taking the law into their own hands, now can we?"

"True. If the man is the father…There is grief, as well as anger, there for some of them."

"Justice will be tempered with mercy for those who deserve such considerations."

With a nod, Duggan turned the horse toward the path and set off at a good clip. Bartell watched for a long moment until one of his men spoke.

"He should have taken some food and supplies. Chances are he'll be looking till first snow fall."

"Nonsense! Did you see the look in his eye? The railroad did not make him a Special Agent without reason." Bartell told the other man. "No, this will see the end of these deaths. I would lay down good hard-earned money on that. From this moment on, remember this, there will be fewer of these railroad deaths in Oklahoma. He is a man who does not stop till the job is done. Good man that one, he reminds me of myself. Come on; let's get this lot to the local jail!"

Duggan heard the booming voice as he rode away and hoped the man's prediction was true. Each jolt of the horse sent waves of pain from his ribs.

He thought of the deaths he had followed these last months and vowed he would, God willing, put a stop to this particular line of death.

That was a promise.

PART I:
Life & Death on the Rails

On a warm day in Oklahoma, workers found an unidentified and nearly nude male body within feet of a rail line. On closer examination, the nature of the bruises showing on the man's remains meant the initial theory would not suffice. A hapless soul hit by a train no longer fit.

Across the state, to hide their crimes, criminal elements dumped bodies along the tracks with throats slit "ear to ear" and skulls "crushed." Passing trains have helped disguise their deeds in the past. This time, however, they were not lucky and the body gets spotted before a train comes through.

Local dogs found human bones and drag them, snarling and fighting over ownership, through the hot and dusty streets of a southwest Oklahoma town. Authorities, eager to close a messy case, look at the bones and quickly determine death by "natural causes."

A local farmer found dead in his yard with his throat cut. So aggressively and deeply made is the incision that it nearly severs his head from his shoulders. Local police surprisingly label it a clear "suicide." The man's farm is within easy walking distance of a busy rail spur.

Across the state, all within easy reach of a rail line, other bodies appear.

This could be the start of a morbid piece of fiction, but it is all too real, and comes straight from the pages of Oklahoma history. It is the other side of history, the wrong side of the tracks if you will, where elusive suspicions might linger. This kind of history is a shadowy place where tales of death, scandal, and murder bob around like an ever-present railroad signal lantern in a mysterious night.

Some will be quick to point out that working the railroad was a dangerous business to quickly dismiss any strangeness in the deaths. The "roads" have always been dangerous and to be viewed with extreme respect and caution. In some periods, including the ones covered in this survey, regulations and safety features taken for granted today were lax or non-existent. Although the railroads often claimed you were in more danger of falling down the home stairs than being hurt by a train,[1] there is little doubt the railroads were, and are, dangerous. They remain dangerous today due to many of the same issues found in the earliest man versus machine encounters: inattention, trespassing, comprised reactions due to intoxication, and a general lack of respect for the large train's speed, power, and lack of maneuverability.[2]

Some might question the possibility of a killer working the lines in early day Oklahoma, but there is ample evidence of such behavior in recent times. In July of 1990, 39 year-old Angel Maturino Resendez, was apprehended for committing murders using the railroad systems as means of transportation and escape.

Illegally riding the rails, he would hop off long enough to commit a murder and then catch the next train out of town. If he could do this in a modern time when trains are not as thriving, common, or as easy to access – what could someone have done in the early years of the 20th century?

Recognizing that the rails were dangerous, obvious wrecks, accidents, and other expected incidents, although numerous and often interesting, are not included in this work. Mishaps occurred frequently: deaf farmers walked into trains, runaway teams collided with oncoming trains, workers were careless, and people were a bit too casual around the new trolley cars, simply fell while riding or while trying to jump from a train.

The railroads built their network of tracks by buying land but sometimes these were in areas where people had no clear paths or where no bridges existed. The rails owned the tracks, the right of ways, easements, and supplies areas where workers might camp or keep handy replacement ties.

Many of the accidents recorded were on the tracks and this was considered trespass because the rail line and its right of way were the property of the railroad company. Although people were discouraged from using the rail lines as a modern 'footpath', the truth was they often used the lines as a sure way of going from point A to B in a time when roads were scarce.

The long rail "road" or the trestles provided a means of getting someplace with greater ease. This would create many problems for both the railroads and the citizens.

The railroad offered one way or another, a steady stream of news for area papers. Often in this survey, the only deaths or accidents recorded appeared to be related to the railroads. Deaths from farther afield in small farming or ranching communities were often rare. Ian Savage noted that between 1905 and 1920, 'the fatality risk per head of population was thirty-five times larger than today." He notes that accidents involving railroads were most often classed as related to some form of trespass.[3]

Consider these as a sampling of headlines dealing with such "normal" incidents:

"Terrible Death: Bert Clay, a Santa Fe Freight Conductor, Perished Under the Whels[sic].

"Body severed by train." The Oklahoman (July 24, 1903): pg.5. The accident occurred in the local rail yard and was witnessed only by two small boys.

"Jumped from Moving Train with Son: Bristow Man and child narrowly escaped death under the wheels." The Oklahoman (Aug. 22, 1905): pg.2.

"Body is Severed: Arthur Reynolds Instantly Killed By A Frisco Engine Yesterday: Failed to Hear Engine" The Oklahoman (Oct.3, 1906).

"Chickasha Man Slain by Train: Slightly Deaf, He Fails to Hear Warning Whistle and is Run Down". The Oklahoman (Dec. 29, 1910): pg. 4.

"Body Sticks on Engine: Is Carried for Almost a Quarter of a Mile Down Track", The Oklahoman (Sept. 21, 1907).

Terrible accidents were sure to happen when tons of powerful machinery and careless, thoughtless, or unlucky people intersected. It may also be true that sometimes the only difference between an accident and a murder was a witness.

THE GOOD OLD DAYS

Oklahoma, before and after statehood in 1907, was a wild and wooly place where thugs, criminals, crooked politicians, and ordinary citizens intermingled. The Law was sometimes scare and not as lawful as it might have been. Gunfights, bank robbery, and outlaw gangs still gave a "romantic" flavor to the land. The 1890's saw poverty, labor, class, and race tensions all mingling with "get rich" schemes. There were also problems with youthful offenders -juvenile delinquents- due in part to several social factors at work in the 1890 to 1930 time period.

One such tale of wild youth was from Choctaw and told of an 11-year-old boy who stole his mother's horse, sold it, and then stole some rifles. When he could not find any game, he turned the guns on a couple of horses in a farmer's field. When arrested, the police and reporters noted, he seemed very unconcerned and seemed to have no feelings about his actions.4

This could be reporter over statement or it could be that this young man was a budding sociopath or psychopath. Experts say that in any group of people there is bound to be at least one person with the potential to become the classic serial killer.

In a society where a person's death – be it from gunshot, accident, murder, war, or lynching was so common – such callousness or anti-social behavior could be expected to emerge.

A NOTE ON RACE AND CLASS

Any historical research uncovers the way things once were – both the good and the bad. At the turn of the 20th century, the United States was greatly influenced by European class structures, emerging philosophies about the "survival of the fittest", a health and wellness craze, and radical ideas about social engineering. Evident in newspapers, pulpits, schoolrooms, and the workplace were often strange mélanges of class, race, sexual, and religious biases.

Many groups came in for their share of prejudice in the early days: Asians, poor and uneducated whites, Europeans who spoke little English, African-Americans, and Native Americans. Unfortunately, in early day Oklahoma, racism was a harsh reality of daily life for most Native and African Americans. Yet, bias and racism when is allowed to flourish soon consumes any to whom the label "not us" can be applied.

Few stories of crimes against Native Americans appeared in the newspapers, and this may be due to their status and their relationship to the Federal Government. The few which do emerge reveal they remained easy targets for the small minded.

Segregated, restricted by various "sun down" laws, and viewed as the first suspect in any crime, African Americans were termed "negroes" (or variations of the word), "coloreds" and often simply "brutes" in the pages of newspapers. To the more socially progressive they were Negroes and to those with other views another word was sometimes used.

Objective reporting, then as now, was often a shallow rooted plant easily dislodged. In the early days, the southern ethos and attitude were very apparent and Oklahoma newspapers often included dire predictions of potential lynching. Sometimes there was the clear hint that this was seen not as a bad thing but an act of justice. Additionally, just past the turn of the century, "night riders," who were possible political or racist agitators, began appearing here and there around the state's smaller communities.

They were attempting to intimidate and influence local events from elections to farmers building coalitions. Similar tactics were well known to be used by Klansman and in fact the KKK by the 1920's would be rampant in many

Oklahoma communities and even in state government.

In retrospect, it is amazing that in a little less than 60 years the first "sit in" of the civil rights movement would occur, peacefully, in downtown Oklahoma City.

Changes were inevitable, if not always mutually comfortable, as the state confronted its heritage of racism in the remaining years of the 20th century. Great strides in racial understanding would be made but it would often be a route mired by cultural conditioning remaining from the previous century.

In our context, an incident in 1902 in Oklahoma City is illustrative of how society responds as society has been taught. Buried in the miscellaneous column called "City In Brief" the sub-title declared, "Made A Gruesome Find." Two "white boys" observed a "colored man" burying something by the river. "Immediately suspicious", the two boys dug up what the man had buried and found the arm of a "colored boy". They instantly assumed the man had committed murder and called authorities. Upon investigating, however, the authorities learned that the arm belonged to a young African American boy who had sadly lost his arm when he had fallen under a train. During this period, it was common for news items related to incidences among African Americans, foreigners, Native Americans, or the "lower classes" to never make it into print or if it did (like this one) to never provide names.5

Issues of class and sexism are also important in looking at these stories and the wider society in which they were set. The poor, the immigrant, the homeless were scourges on the creation of model progressive civic settings, or so many thought. Newspapers overflowed with the activities of the "society", of free speeches and presentations designed to educate and elevate the "lower classes" and to lift them to the highest standards of a "civilized" society.

The good old days had many things to recommend them: small town values, simplicity of lifestyle, neighborliness, patriotism, family, and self-sufficiency.

People are only human. Despite the rosy glasses, however, it has to be remembered that also in the good old days, the poor were ignorant, the homeless criminals, a woman good because she was beautiful, and all 'outsiders' suspect.

CRIMES

In 1900, according to FBI statistics, the U.S. Homicide rate was 1.2 per 100,000. During this period, there were a large number of homeless youth. They frequently used the rails to move about. In fact, so many youth were traveling that a National Curfew Association formed to enforce a curfew in towns all along the rail lines.6

In 1905, for some reason not clearly identified by most researchers, the U.S. Homicide rate rose to 2.1 per 100,000. From 1906 to 1919, there was a steady increase until 1919 when the rate was 7.2.7 It has yet to be determined if these were the result of mere population growth, some spike in murders, or simply reflected improving communication systems for reporting such crimes. This time period of 1900 to 1906 included the great 'muckraking' scandals and a severe economic depression.

With that in mind, the criteria for inclusion in this listing were clearly limited to a particular range of incidents. The criteria were:

1. The incident had to have taken place near a railroad line or facility (yard, service center, etc.);
2. The incident had to have involved wounds to the head ("bashed in", "crushed", etc.),and/or to the throat ("cut ear to ear", "head severed", etc.), or marks that could be interpreted as inflicted before the incident on the tracks;

3. The incident had to be potentially "suspicious" (falling asleep as a train hurtles toward you, placed on track to cover a crime, etc.); or recognized at the time as suspicious.
4. The incident had to be in a locale that appeared to have an unusually high rate of similar deaths.

Here then, are the stories with question marks. These tales beg for further details and a closer look. Here are circumstances, or coincidences, of death that stain credulity to the breaking point. Similar wounds, similar victims, and proximity to rail lines all beg the question: did an early day serial killer ride the rails in early Oklahoma?

PART 2:
STITCHING THE LAND

Oklahoma, before 1907, contained two main territories. It had been the no man's land thought to be worthless with its vast plains of tall grasses. Native populations were moved into the eastern half and the western half, home to migratory tribes and buffalo herds was largely left alone. This state of non-being made it a magnet for outlaw types, murderers, thieves, and others who simply wanted to disappear.

Forced Native American settlement, coupled with a strong European American presence, saw the eastern half develop schools, communities, and a stronger population. Before long it was hoped the "Indian Territory" would become its own state. The central region of the state was the "Oklahoma Territory." Although some sections in the west and south were set aside for various native tribes, or the federal government, they were viewed as part of the "Oklahoma Territory."

It was an exciting time as one of the last frontiers of the "old west" was rapidly coming into line with an increasingly "modern" society. The Indian and Oklahoma Territories could recognize, and often welcome, the warning signs that the times were changing. For others, a land that had been a haven for outlaws and those who needed to keep a low profile, that change would be hard. At the time of statehood in 1907, most major towns had modern amenities galore: telephones, motor cars, passenger trains, trolleys, theater, opera, sidewalks, and many other emerging marvels.

Perversely, people would continue to take a certain pride in the lawless days, perhaps a symbol of how tough they had to be to overcome the situations. Such headlines as "Many Mysterious Murders Make Men Fear 'Dead Man's Gulch' on Old Atoka trail" in the Oklahoman were no doubt just this type of perverse bravado.8

The first railroad into the future state of Oklahoma arrived shortly after the civil war and by 1899 there were twenty-six companies.9 At the time of statehood, nearly 6,000 miles of track spread out across the territories. In 1902, the Choctaw, Oklahoma & Gulf railroad ran extensions from Weatherford on to Amarillo, Texas, south from the Oklahoma City southward to Ardmore, and east to Tecumseh and smaller cities, including the African-American community of Romulus10. That same year, The Santa Fe, charted a daring course from Woodward, Oklahoma down to Quanah, Texas, even though it went through territory already clearly in use by Rock Island, The Orient, and Frisco companies.11

Railroad repair shops, according to early historian Edward Everett Dale, were located in many communities. Some of the most important ones included Shawnee, El Reno, Tulsa, Muskogee, and Oklahoma City with some smaller ones in Enid, Chickasha, and Altus. 12

The major rail lines in Oklahoma from 1900 to 1920 were:
- The Missouri, Kansas and Texas line (known as the KATY). It crossed the Indian Territory (eastern Oklahoma) linking Kansas and Texas in 1872.
- The Atlantic and Pacific (later known as the "Frisco") focused on east to west routes in the region.
- The Atchison, Topeka, and the Santa Fe (or the Santa Fe) moved into Oklahoma in 1887.
- The Rock Island moved into Oklahoma from Caldwell, Ks to El Reno in 1890.
- The Choctaw Coal and Railway Company linked El Reno to OKC in 1892

Several smaller lines also laid tracks but were subsumed by the larger entities or merely adopted as feeders to link remote areas with the major lines.13

The exciting potential for economic growth made it a natural partnership for newspapers to highlight stories related to the travels, plans, and activities of the major railroads. In some instances, the local newspapers served as a public relations arm for the corporations, with large regular columns becoming a feature.

The stories provide insight into many aspects of life in Oklahoma as the railroads took root. In 1906, the Santa Fe expanded into New Mexico according to an article titled "Railroad News".14 The Rock Island found itself in need of labor in 1908 and so it advertised for locations in several Oklahoma areas for men to work at grading, ballasting, and other work. [15] It was probably a slow news day in 1914 when C.M. Sarchet out of Ringling, Oklahoma wrote about the "Queer Mascots" often found in railroad camps. Cats, dogs, and even bantam chickens haunted the camps and some even rode the bumpers of the cars with ease. 16

Life could be dangerous off the tracks as well for those who worked for the railroads. A 1912 story out of Chicago probably made more than one laborer look twice at the woman running the boarding house or the kindly woman giving him an inviting look, or perhaps reconsider his dreams of settling down. *"Modern Lucretia Borgia on Trial"* blared one headline telling of the woman who married several men, and then poisoned them with arsenic. 17

In this research, certain towns play major roles due to their placement along major and minor rail lines and as hubs of settlements.

The earliest rail lines, the MTK, came north out of Texas into Indian Territory in 1872. It moved on to join lines in Missouri and Kansas. Communities in this eastern section of the current state borders included: Atoka, Muskogee, Keystone, Tulsa and Wagoner.[18]

Early rail lines elsewhere in the state included Chickasha (chick-a-shay) originally called Pensee and renamed in 1892. Frederick, in southwest Oklahoma, was established in 1901 as Gosnell, and the name changed in 1902. In 1892, the Rock Island RR arrived establishing it as an important transportation hub.[19]

Oklahoma City, established in 1889 with the land run, was in 1887 first the location of the Oklahoma Station. Around this central core railroads spilled out in every direction. Choctaw, first known as Choctaw City in 1890, is east of OKC and in 1896; named for the "Choctaw Coal and Railroad Company" that arrived in 1896 Enid was established in 1893 as the busy site of the Rhode Island Depot. El Reno, established in 1889, was originally bypassed by one early line, the *Choctaw, Oklahoma, and Gulf* RR (consumed by the Rhode Island) but was eventually developed despite this initial rejection.

Without a doubt, working on early day railroads was a dangerous job. Couple that fact with opening up new territories, various train companies fighting for dominance, and a generally lawless prevailing environment, and the results were sure to be deadly.

EVENTS, NEWS & ACCIDENTS

The romance, excitement, and economic prosperity promised by the coming of the railroads are often hard for contemporary people to understand. Newspapers printed miles of news concerning the comings and goings of railroad workers, surveyors, engineers, and administrators.

The railroad system was a lifeline of economic survival for numerous small towns in Oklahoma. Wooing and keeping rail lines would be crucial to their development in the coming years. The miracle of this fast technology that carried a person to distant places in a short amount of time soon became an accepted part of daily life. Generations would be born hearing the lullaby of the engines as they hurried past on the rails.

"Robbed on Train: Pickpockets did a Good Business on Rock Island Yesterday" The Oklahoman (Jan.23, 1903): pg. 8.
A gang if thieves who had been working the lines from El Reno to Oklahoma had a particularly good day. Using the "rush act" they robbed an insurance man, some visiting business men and others of a least $100.

"Railroad News: General Agent Vickers has Resigned from the Frisco; Shawnee and Katy" The Oklahoman (Feb.18, 1903) pg. 8. A surprising resignation but considering the dangerous condition around the Shawnee dept, possibly not surprising.

"Death of Guy Loughmiller: Frisco Railroad Brakeman Expires at Springfield, Mo." The Oklahoman (Dec. 29, 1902): 6.
On Dec. 24, Chickasha brakeman, 24-year-old Guy Loughmiller, was thrown off balance as he worked by the sudden stopping of a train and another car ran over his legs. Taken to the Railroad hospital at Springfield, Missouri, he died several days later.

"Section Foreman Charged with Fraud" The Oklahoman (Dec. 23, 1904): pg. 3. He had been adding names to the payroll and pocketing the difference.

"Fatally Shot by Frisco Agent At Elgin' The Oklahoman. (Oct. 13, 1906): pg. 1. Sometimes station agents had to protect themselves and in this instance it was deadly.

"Attempt is Made to Wreck Trains: Railroad Detectives Searching for Men who Placed Ties on Tracks." The Oklahoman (July 5, 1907): 1. Unknown criminals were at work near Iowa Park and Lawton where ties piled on the tracks were found. Detectives from the Fort Worth and Denver City Railroad were investigating the episodes.

"Saves Passengers From Fatal Wreck: Bridge Gone, Woman Builds Bonfire and Stops A Train." The Oklahoman (Aug. 13, 1907):10. Story from Kansas City of an incident near Ethel, Missouri.

"Engineer Not Blamed, Road Found Guilty" The Oklahoman (Sept. 22, 1907): pg.1. The finger was pointed at the company for not maintaining the tracks and trains thus causing an accident.

"Hundreds of Tons of Coal Stolen: Sheriff's Department Notifies Chief Special Agent of the Frisco." The Oklahoman (Feb.1, 1908): pg. 5. Over 300 tons of missing coal was reported to the special agent, Samuel Alender of St. Louis. Some of the material had been taken directly from the yards and rails stops in various wagons.

"Two Bulgarians Are Held, Murder Charged: Railroad Employe (sic) is brutally slain at Camp Near Atoka". The Oklahoman (May 28, 1908): pg. 7. Arrested in Atoka for killing a fellow rail worker and then they escaped hopping a KATY train to St. Louis but were caught in McAlester. Strangely, in Duluth, Minnesota Bulgarians figured in a mass murder there in 1906.20

"Fourteen-Year-Old Murderer Not Free," The Oklahoman (Sept. 24, 1908): pg. 4. Out of Tulsa came the story of Frank Rutherford who had taken an axe to his uncle, Shelley Ellis.

"Negro Confesses to Poe's Murder", The Oklahoman (Aug 20, 1909):pg. n.p. from the Arcadia jail came news of a confession that Alex Poe had been killed by fellow rail camp crew member Henry Sanders over a girl.

"The Daily Newspaper" The Oklahoman (Aug.22, 1909): pg. 22. A reprint from the St. Louis republic quoted Arthur L. Street of Chicago in noting that "railroads receive more attention from the newspapers than murders and suicides" and that the "modern newspaper …must hold the mirror up to the doings of the world…Among its functions is to record the effects of causes that have been many days or many months in operation."

"Youth is Victim of Car Accident." The Oklahoman (June 13, 1910): pg. 7. O.R. Bolton, aged 20, attempted to swing aboard a Belle Isle train car and missed. He severed his right leg and badly damaged the other and he was not expected to survive.

"Effort to Locate Train Wreckers," The Oklahoman (Dec.3,1910): pg. 9. Railroad detectives from Sedalia, Missouri investigated an accident caused by "train wreckers" – people who deliberately attempted to slow, halt, or wreck a train for the purposes of robbery or murder.

"8,165,406 Tons of Freight Handled" The Oklahoman (Sept.29, 1911):pg. 11. The gauge of the economy is often the amount of resources moving across the country in response to "supply-and-demand". The KATY showed a 9.07 increase in tonnage, mostly in mining products, in 1911, underscoring the vital role the railroads were playing in the development of the state and the nation.

"Safety First" Lessens Deaths: Practice is New Motto by Frisco Employes (sic) Already is Bearing Results." The Oklahoman (Feb.11, 1912): 26. Risky behaviors of employees were the target in this move and it was incorporated in their "Frisco Rules and Regulations".

"Safety Habit Sweeps Country: Railroad Reports Show Reduction of Accidents Since Last Issue" (April 21,

1912): pg. 17. The Atchison, Topeka, and Santa Fe reported a decrease in deaths and injuries among their employees for the previous year. They reported that in 1911 only two passengers were killed on over 6,000 miles of Santa Fe proper, over 6,000 miles. One was a circus man who had hopped a ride and fell off and the other a passenger who killed another passenger. The Santa Fe was quick to point out that Santa Fe RR fatalities number 88 but that according to newspaper reports "3,374 people met violent deaths in accidents off the railroad right of way".

"Old, But Proud, Woman in Need: Deserted at Station by Son Who Sought Job Elsewhere." *The Oklahoman (July 15, 1912): pg. 7.*
Walter Silver, Frisco Special Agent, was making his Saturday night sweep when he encountered 70-year-old Mrs. John Quinn, "utterly abandoned, homeless." Her 40-year-old son, John, and she had come to Oklahoma City to speak to Anton Classen, president of the "Oklahoma Street Railway. Apparently, he had received word of a railroad position in Fort Smith and had left. Perhaps there had been no funds, or he had left so hurriedly he had forgotten to leave funds, but in any event, his mother was left without money. She expressed a willingness to work, but police thought she might be too feeble to do so and was turned over to the local police matron, Mrs. Sam Bartell (Sam Bartell was an early

U.S. Deputy Marshall, early police officer, and local detective).

"Missing Employee Returns to Die" The Oklahoman (Feb.26, 1913):pg. 12. David Lesser, who had been mysteriously missing for eighteen months, had just returned to his family in El Reno a week previously, when he was killed in an accident in the Rock Island rail yards there.

"Bridge Guard is Killed By Train: Sixteen-Year-Old Youth is Killed by Train on Santa Fe Tracks." The Oklahoman, (July 3, 1913): pg. 7. Eugene Osborne supported his mother and two younger children as a section hand for the Santa Fe and when overtime duty called he answered, despite being tired from a day's work. The hard working youth was hailed as one of the "soldiers of peace" who had died on their posts for the railroads.

"Boy Nearly Torn Apart by Wheels" The Oklahoman (April 15, 1916): pg. 5. Charles Goetzinger, 16, was injured under a slow moving Rock Island train while riding the bumpers. Although taken by ambulance to the hospital, he died before they could operate. The sometimes student at Willard School had recently been employed by the Fremont Foundry. Officials noted that they had had quite a little problem with boys from Willard "hopping" trains. Railroad officers noted that boys had been in the habit of "catching" freight trains at various crossings and riding.

PART 3:
GRUESOME FINDS

PRE-1900, OTHER LOCALES

Another consideration in examining these deaths was the question if they were singular to Oklahoma, or did similar deaths occur in other locations along railway lines. A story in the New York Times of 1894 indicates that using the rail to disguise a murder was not a new idea.21

Noting the early rail lines with deaths recorded in Oklahoma came from Texas that was a natural starting place. What might be found looking south to where the lines began?
1890-1900

A collection of news stories from 1896-1900 in the area of Waco, Texas also provides balance to the types of news and deaths reported in the later time.

Some were clearly heartbreaking accidents, natural deaths and careless decisions. Others, however, seemed, strangely familiar to deaths to be found elsewhere at other time.

Some where clearly early 'urban legends'; the number of infants thrown off trains and reported in shocking prose by local newspapers would have populated a small town. Yet, it did occasionally happen as is illustrated by the story of a skeleton of an infant was found along the MKT tracks in 1896 near Waco, Texas and mirrored by similar finds in later Oklahoma.

Other tales included a "KATY" brakeman killed by a train, an unknown man found dead along the Aransas Pass railroad system, and two years later, a man was killed when run over by a railroad car, while yet another man died of injuries in a rail accident.

The trend was apparently set as the number of serious 'accidents' and deaths increased by 1900 as more were hit by trains, knocked off bridges, or had their throat cut.22

The crew of the Missouri, Kansas, & Texas rail line (KATY) train No. 19 discovered the body of a young man about 20 years of age on the tracks and took the remains to nearby Whitesboro, Texas. It was apparently reported in several north Texas newspapers, including those in Gainesville and Denton. He had been last seen loitering about the KATY Depot. They noted that when caught by the train he was strangely "laying across the tracks, apparently asleep." 23

Death seemed to shadow those who worked or traveled the rails. C.M. Lewis, a Pullman sleeping car conductor, in June 1901 there was a body found dead by the railroad tracks near Waco. He had a bullet hole to the left temple. In the same period, another man, a 55 year old loner named D.A. Harris, died suddenly near the KATY depot. 24

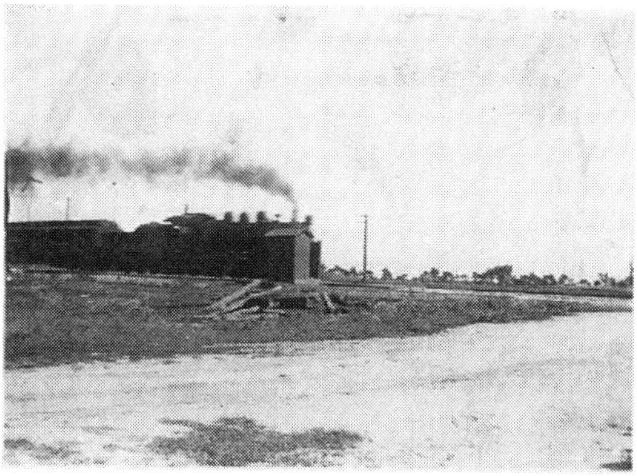

SCENERIOS

He rode the car, swaying slightly as he clutched the door-jamb, looking out the open door at the fields and pastures as they passed. At his feet were the bodies of the two young men who had been in the car when he climbed aboard and they had offered him food, a smoke, and even some water.

Shiftless, lazy louts, they all were worthless anymore. They should be at home helping their parents on farms or tending some business to learn a trade. As the train made a slight curve, braced himself in the door, and he kicked the two bodies out. He watched them tumble down the embankment into the dry grass and knew that the chances were good it would be assumed they had been hit and killed by a train. Trains were such dangerous things, after all.

If he had sons to help him, well maybe the bankers and the railroad men would not have robbed him of his place. Then maybe his wife would have stayed as well.

He hated banks and railroads and that was strange seeing they were responsible for the skills he now used so well. He had become hired muscle to scare off rival companies, farmers, and anyone else they men with the money wanted to be someplace else. He had learned that he might have been a lousy farmer but he did some things well. He also learned he had a taste, maybe even a gift, for this work as well.

Beatings soon became murders and as he honed his skill he learned some deaths were not too closely investigated by the authorities. It was easy to make some deaths look a lot like accidents. If a man was good at his work, and he was, why he might even get away with murder.

PART 4:
MORE GRUESOME FINDS

OKLAHOMA, 1900-1920

In the early years of the century, close settlements were rare and railroads were just starting to look at the region. Early rail companies had established themselves in certain areas but others began to spread out seeking to guess at new areas of growth. Land, rail, and industry speculation were the constant discussion in communities and government.

Of note in regards to these deaths was the fact they occurred most frequently along rail lines. Was this due to the fact news could travel faster that way or because more deaths occurred around the rail lines? Strangely, few examples of deaths came from the further distances leading to suspicions that more might be contributing to these deaths than dangerous machines.

1901

In early October, J.R. Tilley of Weatherford was on his way home when he was permanently detoured. Local ranchers had found his body, seven miles east of Anadarko (in present day Caddo County), snagged in the shore debris in the circuitous Washita River. His attackers had dispatched him with three blows to the head with a blunt instrument. Authorities quickly noted he had been struck deliberately several times. A blood pool was nearby but answers seemed distant in this particular mystery25.

The Chicago, Rhode Island, and Pacific Railroad (in one of its incarnations) ran nearby in several locations east, west, north, and south Anadarko. This story meets the criteria by its proximity to a rail line, a location where a killing might have occurred and a body might be dumped, and an accident assumed.

The next month in the central part of the state, near Wellston, a German baker with a taste for liquor had one too many and paid the ultimate price. Authorities assumed the man had fallen asleep on the tracks. Like Humpty-Dumpty, the railroad crew picked up pieces of the man for over three hundred yards, but there was no putting the man back together.26

Although no one actually saw the death, authorities stated quiet firmly, as they would frequently in coming years, that the man had fallen into such a deep sleep he had been run over by the east-west St. Louis and San Francisco line.

Later that same month, six miles east of Shawnee, along the early Choctaw line, the body of a thirty-five year old man was found, his head crushed, and all but his jeans stolen. He was found with yards of one of the local rail lines.27

Even at this early date, Shawnee was a rapidly growing community with great promise as its cotton and other crops attracted railroads eager to transport lucrative crops. The region's role in early Oklahoma railroad history was solidified when a rail hub for maintenance opened there. It was a boon helping to swell the population and support the east –west and north-west to southeast Chicago, Rhode Island, and Pacific.

In 1901, deaths meeting the criteria were apparently more sporadic but arched from southwestern Oklahoma, turned northeast and then hooked down again angling to the southeast. Although, few deaths meeting criteria occurred in Oklahoma's region, it is interesting to note that prior to this year, in north Texas, other men were also found dead along some of the same rail lines or rail lines feeding into the Oklahoma lines.

1902

The railroads were expanding and the landscape became a tempting morsel attracting entrepreneurs, investors, speculators, and more than a few schemers. Miles of track connected communities to the outside world, new industry was emerging, and the once rough and wild 'badlands' of the soon to be state were becoming 'civilized'.

Major communities developed high levels of culture taming a new urban wilderness with universities, businesses, and opera houses at the same time that cowpokes and farmers were harnessing the potential of the land building an agricultural kingdom. With all that money, land, and power up for grabs, it was a recipe for trouble.

On an April day in Wagoner, a horrible discovery disrupted the verdant spring. In a vacant lot, the body of 24-year-old Will Haynes of Virginia was found, with his throat slashed by a pair of scissors found nearby28. In a sad commentary on the racism of the state at the time, authorities rounded up several "negroes" as suspects who had to be moved to Muskogee to avoid a lynching. There were, however, no clear ties of the men to the murder other than racist fears and fantasies.

Wagoner was in part of the state where the Missouri, Kansas and Texas (called the Katy) had come into the then Indian Territory right after the Civil War. It soon reached from Denison, Texas (and further south) all the way north toward Baxter Springs, Kansas. It expanded until the line actually formed an awkward "U" shape as it moved from Dallas, Denison, Durant, Atoka, McAlester, Eufaula,

Muskogee, Wagoner, and then north into Kansas. Once in the sunflower state the railroad curved back down re-entering Oklahoma near Dewey, moving to Bartlesville, Pawhuska, Luther, and then Oklahoma City. To the south the rail turned west at Dallas and aimed at Wichita Falls before turning north to Frederick, Altus, Elk City, Woodward, and Knowles in the Oklahoma panhandle.

In early August, Shawnee was where J. L. Hodges was found with a crushed head and his body severely damaged. Authorities sent bloodhounds on the trail of the killer, or killers, but they lost the scent at the nearby Choctaw depot.29 Did the dogs and their handlers wander nervously around casting anxious looks down the curving double bars of steel? As the distant train whistled in the distance, did they say what was in their thoughts? Did they wonder, standing there in the shadow of violent death, if the train carried the killer further away each moment?

The trees were turning their fall colors in October, as three fifteen-year old boys died. Killed by a train near Noble, the three were thought to have not been asleep and had simply not heard the approaching train coming around a slight curve. In 1904, their families, or representatives, sued the Frisco charging the boys had been kicked off and had to walk leading to their death.30

SCENERIOS

Jack was a young man and before he had set out to travel the land, he'd been a bit fuller through the body. For all its shortcomings, at home there had been plenty of good food. He was still muscled it was true, but they were now the lean tendons created by lots of hard work and never enough food.

He was also strong; he had to be to make his way as he had for the last year or so. He could jump on the train with ease. He knew he could hold the frame with a sure hand and ride the underbelly for many miles before a railroad bull caught him at some stop.

The danger was that he would grow tired, lulled by the endless rattle of the train along the steel, and lose his grip as muscles finally gave out.

Yet, he had always made it before and so he hustled along the train as it slowed for the grade and pulled himself on. This time, however, his luck ran out.

Losing his grip he fell to the ground and the hard rush of air, a low hanging piece of metal spun him around like a top.

Knocked unconscious in a split second, he never woke as the massive metal wheels carried tons of weight across his body, crushing his limbs, and scattering his mangled body along the line in a long bloody trail.

1903

Railroads were expanding in 1903 and new railroad lines to Shawnee opened April 25. November saw expansion by Frisco into Kansas and the cancellation of a track-laying contract with the long-run Missouri, Kansas, and Texas.31 That summer the Choctaw, Oklahoma & Gulf Railroad had trains headed east that left the Oklahoma City depot at 1:45 a.m., 2:30 p.m., and 10:55 p.m. Westbound trains left at 2:55 a.m., 2:35 p.m. NS 6:20 a.m.32 At year's end, over a thousand miles had been built in the Oklahoma Territory.33

The opening of a newer line into Shawnee, if a killer was at work, should reveal some suspicious deaths in that area….

All the new construction, business, and activity related to the ever expanding iron arterial known as the railroad meant workers. These crews were comprised of regular railroad workers and short timers. Sometimes they were simply displaced or homeless families trying to put together enough to get a fresh start. Sometimes they were criminally inclined, willing to hide the lawless, or had problems with alcohol or drugs making them easy to sway. These set up tent cities where workers would live while they attended to a section of rail line and then move on down the line when the work was completed. Periodically along the lines would be supply camps where rock, sand, iron, and wood could be found to repair sections.

Some of the travelers and victims were young men and young were in demand. In September a small ad declared a need for a "good stout boy" of about 18 years for employment at the Oklahoma Plating works on South Harvey.34 There was a lot to lure young men to the area and a lot to challenge their ability to survive.

Outside of Edmond, 13 year-old John Williams, was injured in what was assumed a fall. Authorities offered the idea he had been riding the undercarriage (called the trucks) of a rail car. This was the metal framework with the axle and the wheels and often afforded a small space where one could ride or cling. His wounds were expected to fatal His family resided in a tent city near the Santa Fe depot.35

Unidentified male's body, his throat sliced, his skull crushed and body dragged under a car, found west of the Choctaw tracks in Shawnee. Attempting to make it appear a suicide his killer (s) had placed a razor in one hand.36

1904

Although the new century was only four years old, there was a lot happening in what would be the economic core of Oklahoma. Oklahoma City was developing at record speed less than twenty years after it was settled by the 1889 Land Run. Epworth University, hotels, multi-storied buildings, hospitals, cathedrals, Shriner's Temple, a two-story MKT depot, were only a small portion of the numerous building projects dotting the city.37

Assumed to have been hit and run over by a train along the Choctaw track east of the Frisco crossing, a man's body was found nearly severed. This also shows the start of the use of the popular, albeit morbid, term of "mangled". Due to the proximity and the ease of using the tracks to hide a crime, it is listed here. Rail lines nearby: Choctaw and Frisco.38

The body of a man identified as John G. Miller, his skull crushed, had been found near Kingfisher on February 28 and he had been last seen by the depot in Chillicothe, Missouri.39

A follow-up to the 1902 death of three 15 year old boys (Joe Rogel, Hugh Morrow, and Daniel Carnahan) who, it was alleged, were struck by a train traveling at a high rate of speed, without any head light, and which did not give any warning by whistle or bell. J. C. Hughes, administrator of the estate of the three boys, filed the suit. The nearby Rail line: Santa Fe. 40

The body of Willie McDaniel was found in a field near Shawnee, not far from the tent camping area near the Choctaw railroad tracks. The boy had gone missing several weeks before, just before a snow storm, and the mother had believed he had "wandered away with the wreckers." The account states, "It is evident that the lad started to the time at the time of the storm, but was blinded and wandered into the field, where he finally froze to death." Exactly what made this fact evident was not disclosed and it is clear from other accounts that surmise was often as good as evidence in many instances.41

John R. Eason, according to police, broke his neck attempting to get on a freight train moving out of the yards. His relatives were thought to be near Fort Worth and Madison, Georgia.42

The skeleton remains of man who had had his skull crushed were found, appropriately enough, along "Dead Man's Creek". Various personal effects were found with the scattered remains. One theory was that the man had been a victim of a robber who had committed crimes about five years before in the area of Vernon. Rail lines: M,T, & K (It apparently may have come down through eastern Oklahoma, across Texas and re-entered western Oklahoma into the area of Frederick). 43

An unlit headlight was blamed for the deaths of G.A. Richards and J.F. Johnston as they used a railway tricycle just outside of Chickasha. The bodies had been "horribly mangled" with one body beheaded and one whose skull showed it had been struck. No answer as to why the men did not hear the train, or jump to safety, was presented. The Rock Island was a nearby rail line. 44

A man had moved into a renter farm and within days found a skull in his front yard and searching a body was found buried in the yard. Authorities believed it to be the body of W.A. Agee and that he had probably been murdered by his nephew, James H. Bratcher. Nearby were the St. Louis and San Francisco and the ubiquitous M, T, K.45

A Lawton 14-year-old named Nora Smith suddenly went missing. She had purchased a ticket at Fletcher where she was attending school and had her luggage checked through to Lawton, but never arrived. Her parents dead, her only family were a sister in Oklahoma City and a brother in Anadarko. The sheriff was notifying all the railroad towns to be looking for her.46

"Evidences of brutal murder ...upon the man's body." His skull reveal an "awful dent" and both his son and son-in-law were arrested. There appeared little motive for murder and he had not been robbed. He had disappeared while working with a construction crew and an axe or hammer might have caused the injury to his head. 47

SCENERIOS

Frank woke in the cold dawn feeling a dozen sharp rocks stabbing him like miniature knives.

He tried to sit up and tasted the rancid remains of the cheap whiskey he had had the night before. He had stupidly lost his money in a card game, decided to walk home, and was following the track so he would not wonder off into the night. His head felt like it was going split apart any minute and he struggled to prop himself up on the cold metal of the rail.

Dizzily the world spun around and he felt more than a little sick. He had to get up. Some sound had him groggily turning around and he realized he was too late. The heavy metal cowcatcher struck him flipping him upwards and then trapping him as it roared on its way.

Screaming in agony, he feels the wheel tear flesh and sever bones, before he is kicked away to roll into the dew covered grass. The sun is just lifting over the trees as he takes his last breath and his blood waters the weeds by the railroad tracks.

1905

The small community of Coretta was located in Wagoner County just north of Muskogee. The body of a man estimated to be about 22 years old was found within 200 yards of a railroad station. He had been seen the previous evening in Coretta and said his name was Osborn. Officials theorized he had somehow become lost and froze to death before he could locate the shelter.48

From Muskogee in I.T. came the story of the deaths of two men, Charles E. Spencer and K.E. Martin, found dead along the railroad tracks at Summit (ten miles south of Muskogee). Identical wounds led officers to the belief they had been murdered and their bodies placed on the tracks.49

Local OKC Police Officer Joe Burnett interrupted someone who was beating W. Menze, a railroad workman newly arrived from Dallas. The officer gave chase but the assailant escaped.50

"Skeleton Found in Hollow Tree" screamed the headline but no one could really be sure just what they were seeing. Was it an arcane Native American ritual, a long concealed murder, or some poor traveler's attempts to keep the animals from the body of their friend or loved one.51 Eufaula was on a major rail line and was a crossroads for mining, forestry, and rail lines from an early time. Once again, this is one included because it is a story that lies in a possible nexus of conflicts and because it is so uniquely strange.

A May 31 episode, near Mcloud and Shawnee, illustrates the dangers that could be experienced in early rail travel and how they could also be escaped. A section foreman, his wife, and three children had taken a hand car to pick strawberries.

A train came upon them and all were able to jump to safety, but not without bruises and one broken wrist. Rail Line for the area was the Rock Island. 52

Joe Churchwell was attacked in the KATY yards in OKC and a worker named Howe said Churchwell had been shot by a "clean shaven" policeman. The local police said they thought there might have been a man impersonating an officer because there was a rail detective with the same last name of "Churchwell." Some trying to settle a score might have been mistaken and shot the wrong man. It also provides a possible reason why someone traveling the rails might have been able to move freely without comment and get close enough to kill.53

Several murders and attacks occurred in the later months of this year. From an unsolved murder in Tahlequah to the big city events.54 "Murder or Accident?" queried the bold headline after the body of P.H. Powers, or Charboneau, was found near the KATY crossing in OKC. He disappeared in route to OKC with two other switchmen in a "single vestibule." The remains being so mangled did not seem to jibe with the idea of him falling and it was noted he would have had to stand in front of the engine to be injured. In fact, the man who collected the remains had assumed the victim had been riding the under carriage (i.e., the trucks) because that was when he usually saw that type of damage. Rail lines: Rock Island, KATY. 55

Sometimes it was hard to identify the good guys from the bad guys. Ex-officer O.F. Hicks was charged with the murder of John Peters in Bartlesville in March. Hicks' body was found on the railroad track with evidence of having been beaten with a club. 56 While in the hub of activity known as Oklahoma Town, another man was beaten death by the railroad tracks.57

1906

Oklahoma City was a growing city, multi-storied buildings were planned, and office buildings, theaters, and parks with entertainments were on the horizon. The city streets were planned in spacious dimensions and on them a visitor might see delivery of goods, traveling business men, and speculators of every type. Families were moving to the city to work in the hotels, banks, schools, and factories.

The railroads were crisscrossing the landscape and establishing hubs, depots, and freight stations. In many ways, Oklahoma City of this time would have been little different than other major cities across the land and that included the shadow of death.

The dead body of a man who worked as a cotton candy vendor in OKC, John Johnson, 21, was found near the river and authorities believed he had been murdered.58 A local legend may even tell of this incident. Many people lived in small hollows and villages to the east. Daily they would walk into town to their jobs.

Not long after this murder, one of these men walked along the river in northeast Oklahoma County, not far from the downtown. His story was shared by a family member.

As he walked he could just see the railroad tracks through the tall weeds where the light caught the metal. The river, more sand the water, chugged by thick with catfish and silt.

As the silver moon shed bright light on the landscape, giving everything a soft blue sheen, the man sensed someone walking beside him. He turned to see a figure, crusted in dirt or some dark shroud, and walking parallel with him in the sand but leaving no tracks.

The figure glowed with a faint dirty blue light, like brief flicker of a match. He hurried but sensed the figure was angling toward and he increased his speed but the other was keeping pace. Finally, running he leaped up an embankment and hauling himself over the bridge, rolled onto the road, and turned to see there was no one on the sand bar.

He had not imagined the ghostly figure. Looking up and down the silvery landscape, however, he could see only his own footprints in the silver blue sand.[59]

Local legend preserves some stories but many others are simply lost. Not all stories are preserved in local legend, or if they were, they have been forgotten. Forgotten in the vast quantity of events over the years, the stories fade to mere statistics and then simply fade.

A woman's scream cut through the night with the piercing quality of real terror.

Without thought, the man hurried to the source of the sound. Dashing down poorly lit streets and past dark alleyways, he did not think that bounders might be waiting or that footpads would be hiding in the shadows. He simply responded, immediately and heroically, to the sound of a woman in fear and distress.

A woman struggled with her assailant on a street corner. Soon the two men were struggling. This time the 'good guy' did not win and the result was a dead body placed on the tracks to cover the crime. The woman had hurried away to fetch local police officers but it was too late when they returned.60

It was a warm early summer day near Davis with the bees humming and birds snatching bugs out of the clear warm air. On his way to tow, the man noticed the dogs were playing with something, growling and running around in a fine frenzy.

Must have found some old soup bone, he thought, *or the remains of dead animal.*

As the man neared the competing tangle of dogs, he saw clearly what they were worrying. "My God!" he cried and reached out to take the item. Snapping jaws and growls ignored he tore off his shirt and wrapped the human remains up tight. Gagging a little, he hurried off to get the authorities.

A child's body was uncovered on May 17 near Davis in the remains of a grading camp. Also found by local dogs, it was later determined that the child had been dead only about ten days.

The body of an unknown young man, aged about 20, pinned between a flat car and a pile of logs was found along the Santa Fe in Oklahoma City yards.

One theory was that he had climbed into the car and was killed as the logs shifted in movement. Although it was early June, he wore a "heavy blue coat."[61] The first of several such accidents and some are distinctly strange and even suspicious.

Missouri resident Albert Kennedy's headless body was found in a berry patch near Warren in late July. Authorities believed he had been lured away from the Leavittsburg depot, robbed, and left for dead. The separation of body from head was thought to be the work of four legged predators.[62]

THE PRIESTER CASE (1906)

July in Oklahoma can be sweltering, still and resemble an oven or a windy blast furnace. It was on a July day that a freight brakeman working the Frisco line at Francis, I.T. noticed a strong odor from a wheat car on its way to Blackwell.

On investigation, he discovered the body of 8-year-old Harry Priester, who had been abducted about a week earlier.

The find revealed, in one corner of the car, what was graphically called a "mass of mangled flesh." The report stated it looked as if the young boy had been "mashed by a railroad train and then picked up and thrown into the car."

A news account from Ada clarified that his head had been crushed, his neck broken, his body was semi-clad and so much blood had flowed that it had soaked through some four feet of the wheat onto the rails themselves.[63]

It was further reported he was last seen talking to an "oddly dressed man supposed to be a tramp.[64]" Police indicated they had a "slight clue" that led back to a man in Tulsa.

About two weeks after the body was found, an indignant article, "Sold the What: Car in Which Murder Was Perpetrated is sold for flour" (Oklahoman, July 21, 1906, pg. 2) appeared in the newspaper. It claimed that the wheat, in the car with the dead body, had been sold for flour! The father was outraged and people horrified.

Soon it was acknowledged people had donated money to help defray investigation costs stating. The father assured the public: "I believe I have information that will lead to an arrest and conviction."

On July 22, 1906, "Frisco Denies Charge Wheat Car Was Sold" (pg. 4) in response to stories of the blood soaked grain being callously sold for profit. The information that the wheat would not go to the mill but be disposed of in some respectful manner, was a public relations message. The railroad investigator was also certain that they would, "have evidence enough in time to cause the arrest of the guilty persons who killed the boy."65

Less than one month after the finding of young Priester's body, news papers declared that Tulsa law enforcement had the killers....or did they? The report, written in inciting prose, stated a confession and a "strong chain of circumstantial evidence points to the prisoners as the guilty ones."

Given the known racist attitudes during this time among many in Oklahoma, the veracity and quality of the "confession," as well as the "circumstantial evidence" must be questioned. Subsequent actions suggest that they may have provided easy scrape goats to quickly resolve outcry over the death of the young boy.

Last seen, the original story reported, young eight year old Priester had been in the company of a man, a tramp, but it did not indicate the man was African-American. Apparently local papers and citizens of the day were quick to apply labels as to race.66

Did young Priester have an accident 'skinny dipping' in the nearby water tanks? Was he struck by a train, or car, and his body hidden in the wheat car in fear? Was he attacked and assaulted by the mysterious tramp?

Questions to which there may never be any answers…another mysterious death along Oklahoma tracks.

Other Cases

From the Tulsa Democrat also came the story of three young men aged, 27, 15, and 12 killed on the Frisco tracks. Without identifying the source, the paper asserted the boys had been intent on walking to Oklahoma City and, growing tired, had simply fallen asleep on the tracks. The train rounding a curve did not see them, a problem reported in several deaths by train. Dead were 27 year old George Reynolds, Harry Brown, 15, and possibly John Reynolds, 12. 67

The next story is very much one to make a person pause and consider how deadly even small things can be. A Frisco track gang member, stationed at Cache, near Lawton, was found dead. Authorities determined he had drowned in "two or three inches of water". There were no witnesses, however, but two other "comrades" were reported to have been fishing just a little way down the river at the same time.68

Just five days later, a small boy by a Rock Island passenger train five miles east of Oklahoma City. Decapitated, one limb torn off, his identity was totally unknown. Strangely, and perhaps significantly, the 6 a.m. train's engineer reported seeing "the boy lying face down on the track, but it was then impossible to stop the train." The question arises, was the body already dead and placed there to, once more, hide a crime?69

Other killings occurred that clearly were not accidents. A 74-year-old man, G.H. Pollock, of Iowa, was found near the Rock Island tracks near Lawton. Since he was carrying a large amount of cash police suspected robbery and murder.70

An incident with even more dire overtones occurred in early October. A young man's naked body had turned up alongside the tracks in Amarillo, Texas.71 Authorities indicated that, from the head wounds, an axe or a knife had attacked him.

His clothes were located in a boxcar found nearby and from evidence there it was the likely site of the killing. Local citizens quickly collected a sizeable reward. Within days, the victim was identified as Earl Dockery of Oklahoma.72

SCENERIOS

Robert woke in the cold dawn feeling a dozen sharp rocks stabbing him like miniature knives. He tried to sit up and tasted the rancid remains of the cheap whiskey he had had the night before.

He had stupidly lost his money in a card game, decided to walk home, and was following the track so he would not wonder off into the night.

His head felt like it was going split apart any minute and he struggled to prop himself up on the cold metal of the rail.

Dizzily the world spun around and he felt more than a little sick. He had to get up. Some sound had him groggily turning around and he realized he was too late.

The heavy metal cowcatcher struck him flipping him upwards and then trapping him as it roared on its way. Screaming in agony he feels the wheel tear flesh and sever bones before he is kicked away to roll into the dew covered grass.

The sun rose over the trees as he breathed his last breath and his blood waters the weeds by the railroad tracks.

1907

The year was to be historic as people waited for the forthcoming entry of the twin territories into the union as a single state. The hopes, dreams, and political work of many years were finally bearing its fruit. The "Indian Territory" with its many schools, churches, mines, forests, and communities and the "Oklahoma Territory" with its rangelands, farms, and wide-open spaces would unite in a marriage of opposites determined to make a success of the deal.

Elsewhere things simply continued as they had been as men and women worked and struggled to make a living. They looked forward to payday and to their breaks from the hard labor. Drinking, partying, and generally have a 'good time' are not the sole prerogative of modern society. In certain eras, choices could involve more danger than in others due to crime levels, contaminated drinks, and disease.

Over near Harrah, east of Oklahoma City, events revealed how unlucky or dangerous a little fun might be for a person. His companions did not know the man who died very well. He had apparently not been a talker, but the men thought he had a son in Illinois, and one serving as a midshipman on the battleship Illinois. He died in his bunk in a section house after a bout of heavy drinking. When he failed to haul out that morning, his crewmates left him in his bed to nurse his sore head but surprisingly they found him still there when they returned. The coroner declared he had probably died in a drunken stupor and offered no additional explanations as to the cause.73

The Rock Island lines were a wild and tough bunch of men apparently. They crop up in numerous stories of violence during these early years. One man also bore an appropriate moniker. Mike Meany assaulted J.V. Wegienek in the Chickasha Rock Island yards and then followed it up by assaulting him to a local restaurant with a razor. Onlookers stepped in, took the razor, and held Meany down until the arrival of the deputy U.S. Marshall, E. S. Burney.74

The wife of a farmer in northeast Oklahoma County was walking the edge of a pond near Harmony school. Wrapped in newsprint was a human skull, and with clear memory of the recent notorious missing person and murder of Mr. James R. Meadows, she hurried it to the police.

Meadows had disappeared and, in the parlance of the day, excitement much comment in the area. Last seen at the vicinity of Kentucky and "B" street he had seemed to simply vanish. An illicit affair came to light that convinced a jury a local waterworks man, Rudolph Tegler, had shot Meadows through the heart on June 4, 1907. A lengthy and dramatic investigation began followed by a trial that would drag on for several years (see the book *Tales of Hell's Half Acre*).75

Into this unsettling time came the skull, or skulls, found around the county by apparent jokers.

One was clearly a man's skull, claimed ex U.S. deputy Marshall Sam Bartell. He further claimed it revealed in the bullet hole piercing the white bone.76 A month later, practical jokers confessed to the placement of this skull or another along a road in the Spencer area.77

Meanwhile, the saga of the Priester case dragged on in Tulsa. Eight year old Harry Priester, it will be remembered, had been found dead in a grain car on July 5, 1907. The case brought to the forefront the simmering racism of the time rose to the surface. Local police had been quick to grasp some local men as the culprit, but when their case came before the grand jury the circumstantial evidence had simply not stood.

Strangely, the father was said to be clinging to a theory that his son had been killed near his home in west Tulsa by falling timber.

How his "near naked" body was tossed in a freight car – in transit to Houston by way of Blackwell - was apparently unexplained and uninvestigated.78

On a cold February day in Oklahoma City, the body of another unidentified young man was found "strewn" along the tracks near California Avenue. Although no one witnessed the event, it was determined he was a tramp who had tried to board the train and lost his footing.

Nearby were Switchmen M.S. Berry and F. Boyd heading toward the depot saw something dark on the tracks and thought it was a dog. They expected it would become frightened and leap away as the engine neared. Nearing the object, they saw it was a man but they were too late to signal the engineer and the engine passed over the body. There were no marks or identifications on the body. Yet again a case of an apparent sleeper who does not move out of the way as the train approaches.79

In what may be an example of the old adage, "what goes around comes around", P.J. DuBois, a painter well known to local police and on bond for forgery, met with his own death about 4:00 in the morning crossing a bridge over Lightening Creek in OKC. Authorities assumed that he was coming home from his work in Capital Hill and was hit on the south side of the bridge. His body, with skull fracture and broken ribs, was found along the bank.80 In 1904, DuBois had choked a boy, 12-year-old Joe Dishman, when the boy knocked a cigar out of his mouth. Cries of alarm, "He is killing him," caused police to hurry to the scene. Officers found him still in front of the Blue Front Saloon choking the boy81

It was a year for killing and hiding the body in trains, along tracks, or in some similar way conceals a dreadful activity. A man was held for murdering a farmer in far northeast Oklahoma. Dewy was a prominent line on the MTK as it sped out of the region headed toward Coffeyville, Kansas. The killer attempted to hide his crime by hiding the body on the tracks.82

Later that same month, near Henryetta a man was shot to death and the killer again tried to cover their act in a convenient and handy manner. D. J. Aubry, a coal miner had been shot by unknown assailants and then his body placed on the Frisco tracks where it was "horribly mutilated when struck by a train." The trainmen's claim the body was already dead was verified with the discovery of the bullet wound. 83

Present day Oklahoma has been, since the mid1950's, 'football mad'. In these early years of the 20th century, however, the fever was all for baseball. Team sprang up in numerous towns and competition was often quite fierce. Local heroes emerged then, just as they do today, to attract crowds, wagers, and attention. Former baseball player and Enid real estate agent, Bert Madden had mysteriously disappeared several months prior while traveling in Denver. The mystery was only deepened when his body was found in the corner of a box car in Sioux City, Iowa. Nothing had been heard of him for three weeks until finally his body was found. Undisclosed evidence indicated a violent death.84

George Hall of Fay, Oklahoma was the lad who did "not awaken when whistle blows" and was struck by a train near Lawton. The "whistle of an approaching passenger train awakened him" but apparently it was too late for him to escape and he was thrown from the track by the impact. His injuries were believed to be fatal. The account does not specify how the authorities obtained their knowledge, from witnesses or from the young man, before he died.85

Echoing the Priester case from Tulsa was a case every parent can understand as their greatest fear. A twelve-year old boy, Roy Hadley, went missing from Pawnee while in the company of an unknown man on April 23. The father believed his son had been abducted by this man and brought to Oklahoma City. Descriptions of the man said he was tall, with a dark complexion, a black mustache, and a small beard wearing a dark broad brimmed hat and dark clothes.86

Another case of shifting lumber was said to be the cause of the death of an unidentified teen, but questions suggest perhaps more was at work than pure happenstance. A 14 year old boy's decomposed body was found as teamsters were unloading a lumber car. Dressed in a blue shirt, overalls and wearing a badge of Sweden, he was obviously traveling to find work or connect to his family. Death was attributed to the piece of wood piercing his heart.

Strangely, the body had its arms folded and authorities suggested he had fallen asleep. Surely this was a bizarre sleeping style, especially for a young man with all his faculties? His possessions appeared to consist of only a book of palmistry and a testament in his pockets.87

Brakemen were definitely in a dangerous line of work as they railroads crisscrossed the land. Ralph A. Rowe, a 24-year-old Santa Fe brakeman who disappeared June 25 from a moving train was found floating in the South Canadian. The back of his scalp revealed a four inch long cut and a fracture of the skull but authorities could not say if this was caused by an accidental fall or a deliberate attack. There seemed be a discrepancy in the amount of money he was thought to be carrying.88 Traveling south from the center of the state-to-be saw a brakeman attacked in Norman. His body showed clear signs of a fracture indicating he had been struck by something.89

Along the watery dividing line between Oklahoma and Texas, the Red River, a body was found that summer as well. It was suggested he had fallen, or been knocked off, the bridge. 90 Atoka, crossroads of old bandit trails and outlaw routes, was often a place of mysterious deaths, headless bodies, and unsolved crimes. It was home to the notorious "Dead Man's Gulch" with stories of strange deaths, mysterious bodies, and buried treasure going back some forty years or more.91

Across the state, what was it about Chickasha that led to so much violence there over the years? The unidentified body of a man found between Oklahoma City and Chickasha with ears cut off, was followed a week later by several arrests. Based on investigations by the Frisco Agency Special Agent Thompson, five men, were being held and charged with murder: George Wyche, Lee Cockran, Claude Hileman, Will Andrews and Jim Johnson. Andrews was the brakeman and the one who found the body.

Andrews said he had worked for the railroad since February and his home was in Mobile, Alabama.

Like an early day soap opera, the story lingered in the news for a long time. New threads and rumors cropped up and then disappeared with some regularity. In 1906 it seemed a young man named Wilbur Gunreth, and an unknown young man may have been mixed up in the grisly events. They were, claimed unnamed sources, "run off" from their home in September. No explanation was found in print as to why they might have been chased from their homes. It was also believed that there was a connection between the later murder of Wilbur Gunreth and the killing of the unknown man found in a Frisco box car ten days prior in Chickasha. Sheriff Harrison of the OKC police force, and Sam Bartell, ex-U.S. Deputy Marshall, ex-OKC Police officer, and now manager of the Oklahoma Detective Agency, were in a race to get into each other's way in solving this tangled case. A foreman and his sons were kept in jail for ten days without charges as people attempted to identify the unknown man's body.92

Meanwhile, around the state bodies littered the landscape, as down around Ardmore, a rancher was found on the tracks.93 An elderly worker was found murdered, by the usual blunt instrument, in a coal pit near Dawson.94 Near

Shawnee, a 20 year old was found dead by the trestle and an accident was assumed.95

In September, Yukon man, 60-year-old Herman Kentz, fell 20 feet breaking his neck on the R.I. trestle near El Reno. Once more an opinion of events seemed just as good as facts for closing a case. Returning home too late to catch the passenger Kentz and another passenger had hopped a freight train and exited it to walk the last distance into town. He fell, the paper reported, and died instantly.96

Local dogs found human bones and drag them, snarling and fighting over ownership, through the hot and dusty streets of the southwest Oklahoma town of Frederick. Authorities, eager to close a messy case, simply look at the bones and determine by some mystical means that the death was by "natural causes." 97

As fall deepened across the state and the harvests were coming to a close, railroad cars were shipping goods, and there was a flurry of activity to transport material to markets. Early October the mangled body of C.L. Cardwell, a Frisco fireman, had been found on the Rock Island tracks near Enid. The first assumption, as it often seemed to be in these cases, was the man had wondered onto the tracks in a "drunken stupor." In this instance, a Rock Island engineer gave testimony that he saw, at about that same time, two men suspiciously "crouching in the grass near the tracks."98

Near Oklahoma City, a Canadian man was found near the Shawnee tracks in December with few identifying papers on him. It was suggested he was a rail worker, a salesman, or a just a lone man traveling.99 Further east, A.J. Ruyle, a coal heaver in Pittsburgh County near McAlester, was found lying dead in front of a rail coal car. Murder was declared once the coroner said he had been dead before being hit by the train and his body placed near the tracks in such a manner as to cover the crime.100

SCENERIOS

Pete hoisted himself on to the train and climbed to the catwalk atop the cars. He braced himself there, swaying as the car rolled over the land.

He'd been stealing a ride for months now, jumping on and off where the train had to slow down to make a curve. It was near the road that led to the farm and easy enough to do.

The train slowed down as it headed into a series of gentle curves, his signal to climb down and get ready to jump off. It would have worked if the embankment hadn't given away during a short rain burst that totally reconfigured the slope of the land.

Instead of jumping off to roll away from the heavy wheels, it now sloped steeply back, and was damp enough to rob him of any purchase. Instead of a safe landing, it spit him right back against the huge wheels as they grasped the steel of the rails.

It was the last ride Pete would steal on that train or any other.

1908

Several railroad bridges around eastern Oklahoma City have legends of numerous reported and unreported dead bodies found beneath them. Some are family legends passed down recounting how a relative had been walking the rails that morning, saw a dead body, and by that night the clearly dead person had been removed but not by authorities. How many more people might have lost their lives by bandits, killers, and train accidents that never saw the news page is anyone's guess. In January, an unknown man was last seen "loitering" at the station and ordered away by an officer, only later to discover his body at the Noble and Santa Fe streets. Authorities believed he had been "stealing" a ride.101

From El Reno came the story of a headless, skeletal body, thought to be the prosperous local farmer, John Sparks. The man had disappeared Jan. 17, 1907.102 Finding headless bodies is not uncommon due to the natural process of predation. The head is easy to remove by small animals and be carried away from the rest of the body. Sometimes, however, it was more intentional. While researching this work so many stories of headless bodies were uncovered a manuscript, tentatively called "Headless in Oklahoma," was briefly considered. Beheading someone remains to this day one the most valuable means of reducing quick identification and is still favored by criminals.

Was it a crime or wasn't it a crime – only the perpetrator knew for sure.

Out of Wynnewood came the tale of a local cowboy, Richard Harris, who discovered a stick of dynamite near the Santa Fe tracks near the Washita River. It was lying inside the track in such a manner that a train going over it might have ignited the stick. Adding to the mystery was the discovering of a mattress along the track, "as though hurled from a train." It bore blood, human hair, and pieces of brain matter. Constables George Harrison, Thomas Livingston, and others searched but found nothing more than a pillow some 400 feet away.[103]

Charles Cooper's badly beaten body, his skull hit at least six times, was found near Rush Springs. Although alive when found, and naming his assailants as Jack Lawson and Jim Roundtree, he died without being able to answer any further questions. No men by that name were located in the area. It was reported that after the operation to save his life, he roused only enough to repeat: "*Let me up Shorty – help me.*"[104]

Further away, the body of T.R. Weems was found near the tower at the Frisco-Santa Fe crossing in Holdenville. His relatives admitted he had a problem with morphine use but was "sunny and cheerful." They were not willing to say he had committed suicide, and the authorities were not sure it was murder. A short time before, the man had been in both Lawton and Chickasha. This tale is included since both of these communities appeared to be hazardous to one's health in this era.105

Seeing patterns of possible nefarious activity in some o these deaths was recognized by contemporaneous investigators as well. Family members often knew someone was at fault but sometimes their claims were ignored as merely the cries of the grief stricken:"Father of missing boy alleges Frisco trainman murdered him....declared a headline in the *Oklahoman* (pg. 12 July 5).

Two other incidences of that time are potential matches for the criteria of odd railroad deaths from central and northern Oklahoma. Simon Love, a Delaware Indian, was found dead along the Iron Mountain railroad tracks. Although authorities first determined he had been struck and killed by a train, additional evidence came to light that he had been robbed and murdered.106

"Body of Missing Man Found: Hone One As A Suspect." The Oklahoman (Dec. 10, 1908: pg. 7. Heavy blows to the face and a headshot, eliminated suicide in the death of missing Stigler man, Thomas Baker. Last seen in the company of friend, Thomas Williams, he had gone to hunt in the Pruett valley woods. A cousin, Will Baker, working on a crew to build a road, discovered his body.

A romantically inclined reporter said poetically that 'death's veil' closed over this case in a shroud of mystery. Found alongside the main Santa Fe track, just north of Grand Avenue in OKC, the body of a middle-aged man. Although he had a crashed skull, broken neck, and left ankle mashed with signs a car had run over it, no skin was broken. Due to the lack of abrasions or cuts, railroad men were reluctant to say a train had hit him. In addition, there was no identification on the body, which led some to think suicide, but others suggested a robber or assassin.[107] Moreover, even visiting could be dangerous as one man from Tulsa discovered. William Smith was just visiting when he had his throat cut by an unknown assailant who subsequently got away.[108]

Sometimes, despite the best efforts of railroad people, telegraph workers, police, and newspapers unidentified bodies remained just that. An unidentified body had been found and W. H. Zwick, the Coroner, had hoped for some identification, but although a Santa Fe agent had been investigating, no name had been found. Not surprisingly, the inquest determined the dead man had come to his death by being run over by a train.109 Conversely, sometimes names were learned but that was about all that ever became known. The Deep Fork Creek ran near the Belle Isle interurban car line near 43rd street in northwestern Oklahoma City. A body was found on a Sunday morning thought to be that of a C.A. Applin, address unknown. A Belle Isle conductor the Friday before said the same man had been intoxicated and the conductor had put him off the car. Police "theorized" he had wondered into the water and some misfortune had befallen him.110

1909

Once again January was a good month for bodies to be found. A body found along the Frisco tracks, one mile west of Frisco near Keystone, early morning revealed a cut throat and a large hole in the head. Due to some papers in a pocket the body was thought to be D.D. Achley. A man of that name and description was living at the Kentucky House in Tulsa and had a mother who lived in Owens, Oklahoma.111

Summer time is generally a time for frivolities, 'play parties' and other enjoyable past times. For some, it is something else entirely. Discovered near Muskogee, in the lower KATY yards, in about July of 1908, was the dead body of an unidentified man. An inquest determined he had died from a bullet wound. Six months later, the "remarkably preserved" body remained, was still around and standing in a coffin stored in local morgue. The coffin featured a small glass lid in the cheap wood to aid identification if it ever came. 112

Prank, criminal activity, or something else resulted in Johnny Clouette, aged 13, being featured in the local news. The boy was the victim of a pair of young men who mysteriously disappeared after tying him to a tree and gagging him, east of the Santa Fe tracks near the town of Capitol Hill. Clouette was the son of a Frisco brakeman and after his ordeal could only say that he had been playing behind the Frisco yards when two young men, about 18 jumped out and grabbed him.113

Yet, another of the headless in Oklahoma makes its appearance in the spring. The man's body was found with throat cut "ear to ear" near the oil field west of Muskogee. The paper indicated he had been dressed poorly, which they interpreted to mean he was either a tramp or a well driller. Police believed his death had been a robbery-motivated homicide.114

In late May, a fishing trip ended with another headless body along the rail tracks near McAlester. A 13-year-old McAlester boy, Guy Roe, was found on the railroad tracks, either "fell off a train or was struck on the track and run over." His father was in Arkansas at the time burying his mother and no answers appeared in print as to why the young man was not with him.115

Local bath-house proprietor, Dee Brooks, was found murdered and his body laid on the Frisco tracks to cover the crime. Clarence Young was shortly arrested for the dire deed and on Aug. 5, 1909 a follow-up article "New Move in Brooks Case" (The Oklahoman; pg. 1) provided more information that additional persons had killed the man.116

Near Chickasha on August 28 came the news that a Rock Island freight train crew, working near Waurika, had found an unidentified body's remains scattered up and down the tracks. First found were blood on the tracks and then a "blue eye, with the pupil staring upward" and bloody remains were found over a six hundred yard span of rail117.

An accident is just an accident unless one has a suspicious mind and a writer often has to have such a warped way of thinking. A report from Tulsa told of a rail car inspector who neglected to flag the car he was inspecting for the KATY railroad. The result was almost his entire body was crushed and he died about an hour later. Talk about your last worst, or cover up a robbery?118

From Chickasha came the tale of a well dressed young man, about 21 years old, emaciated, and shot through the head and had his skull crushed. At first assumed a suicide, the placement of balls in the revolver indicated he could not have killed himself. He had sent a woman in Chicago money based on a money order in a pocket. The condition of the body indicated he had been dead about seven months (his death would have been then about February 1909).119

A similar case occurred later. In the underbrush along the Washita River, near Chickasha, with its head crushed and body mangled, another body was found. Thought to be A.R. Synder who disappeared in April, the body had only an express money order stub on which to base the identification. He had left Lawton in debt, with a woman, and considerable money on his person. The woman returned to Lawton later.120

Police surmised that the body of an unidentified man found in the Arkansas River had been a station agent at Midland Valley at Panama. The man had disappeared and in the subsequent investigations, his accounts found short.121

From Muskogee came the account of a Sallisaw farmer found with his throat cut and items missing from his person. 122 A Sapulpa woman found with her throat cut after an assaulted by an unidentified man. She had been able to fend him off until people nearby heard the scuffle, but in the furor the man escaped into the darkness.123 While over near Muskogee, James Fuller, was arrested for the murder of Charles Blade of Aurora, MO. Nearly cutting his head off, authorities claimed a streetcar (a smaller rail system) in the suburbs was at fault. The assumption was initially the man had been drunk and had fallen asleep on the track. Further inquiry uncovered Fuller was a hack driver who seen quarreling recently with the victim. When this was learned, it was assumed he had placed the body on the tracks to hide the crime.124

SCENERIOS

Claude tossed the luggage out the door as the cars slowed down to a crawl. Usually they operated out of the depot but lately the law had ticking its nose in a little too much. He and the others had come up with this plan instead.

On a slow curving grade the train had to reduce its speed or tilt over and there was a nice deep ravine where Johnny could wait with a wagon. This haul was good, he thought, as he tossed out a mail bag. Claude eyed the boxes of merchandise on its way to Dallas and saw money in those petticoats. Ladies in some sporting houses he knew would pay top dollar for those pretties.

A carton of dishes he overlooked, too heavy and sure to break, but he grabbed a box that looked like it held some linens and tossed them toward the ravine.

He saw Johnny run out and gather the sack, the boxes and the luggage. He tossed a wave and then swung himself out to roll into the weeds just before the train finished the curve. He was already in the wagon and moving away when the train gave a whistle as it train speeded up and headed south.

1910

January with its cold weather was not a good time be stealing a ride on the railroad. The dead body of a boy of about 18 years of age was found in a box car. Police assumed the young man had died of natural causes while illegally riding the car.125

The dead body of a second year law student attending the University of Kansas in Lawrence was found under the Union Pacific railroad bridge at Bonner Springs. It was unknown if Earl Gregory, of Guthrie, Oklahoma, had died from drowning, fall, or mishap. Seen alive just the night before when he told a friend he was walking to nearby Baldwin.126

After months of tentative identification, speculation, and great mystery, the body of a murder victim was laid to rest in a pauper's grave. Found in Chickasha in a box car from Oklahoma City, was the body of man with his ears missing. Over 15,000 people had viewed the body in the past months. Despite several false identifications, the body remained totally nameless.127

Three previous bodies had been found in the region of Chickasha had been similar mysteries. One body was found with a bullet hole in his skull on the bridge over the Wichita. A skeleton with a bullet hole in the skull had been found on the banks of the Washita. The third body had its ears cut off and now another body was found near Chickasha.128

Mysteries however can seem to simply float where they will and this was the case when workers from a local sand company found a body floating in the Canadian River. Due to the high level of decomposition no autopsy was possible and the local authorities ordered the remains buried as soon as possible. The body was that of a man weighing 150 pounds, red-hair, aged 45, and with two fingers missing from his left hand.129

Found along a Frisco track was the body of Marvin Bowly or Boyles, with his skull cracked and bearing two strange holes. Although he was known to have been carrying money, authorities were unable to find any money on him, and assumed he had been robbed.130

Some train lines had suffered more than their share of lawsuits, accusations, and comments about their level of safety. The Frisco was one line that took a proactive role in tightening the workings of their railroad company and its subsidiaries. A Tulsa carpenter had been found dead on the Frisco tracks by a rail crew, the train having passed over his chest and both arms, but Frisco was not silent when the claims were reviewed by local law. As a result, the railroad was cleared, and the incident declared an accident.131.

SCENERIOS

Pete hoisted himself on to the train and climbed to the catwalk atop the cars. He braced himself there, swaying as the car rolled over the land. He looked at the dark sky in the west and thought it would be a bad day with a storm like that on its way.

He'd been stealing a ride for months now, jumping on and off where the train had to slow down to make a curve. It was near the road that led to the farm and easy enough to do.

The train slowed down as it headed into a series of gentle curves, his signal to climb down and get ready to jump off. It would have worked if the embankment hadn't given away during a short rain burst that totally reconfigured the slope of the land. Instead of jumping off to roll away from the heavy wheels, it now sloped steeply back, and was damp enough to rob him of any purchase.

Instead of a safe landing, it spit him right back against the huge wheels as they grasped the steel of the rails. For Pete, it was a very bad day indeed.

1911

Ironically, two news articles appeared in this year touting the new safety focus of railroads. Nationwide railroads, especially the Frisco and the Santa Fe, were quick to proclaim how much their safety regulations were improving conditions for workers and the public.

Conditions on the cars may have improved but the yards and tracks still appeared a killing field. Claud Johnson of Dougherty, Oklahoma was found in the Santa Fe yards with his head split open and was thought to have died instantly with his body placed on the tracks to hide the crime.132

Physical faults are often something people seek to hide to avoid laughter or pity. Unfortunately these identifying marks are all that is left to name a victim. One young man hit and killed by a train had a permanently black toenail and it was this feature that allowed his grieving family to place a name on the body found near Tulsa.133

Thought to have been walking home a Mr. and Mrs. Boatwright, Weleetka, Oklahoma, were attacked. The wife survived the vicious initial attack with four bullet wounds to her head and three in her arm. Although bloodhounds were used no trail was found.134 A few months later near McAlester a Native American was found dead on the tracks in a suspicious manner and two men, with knife wounds, were arrested in conjunction with the investigation.135

The long running mystery from Chickasha, the body of the man with his ear snipped, was apparently solved as a man identified the body. Mystery remains as to who had done the deed or why the ear had been cut.136

1912

There is often no surer witness than the one who was not there. They can clearly identify incidents, provide motives, and describe the actions related to events they never actually saw. Some call this fictional writing, others call it police work, and still others just call it haphazard reporting. Whichever applies, newspapers often produced dogmatic statements about events no one actually witnessed and shared those certainties with their readers. Often the claims were made by local law, coroners, or witnesses.

A witness to the aftermath might say "well there was a man who fell off the cars once a couple of years ago; maybe that is what happened here." Whisper of pencil across newspaper pad and the story is off and running. Maybe that is what happened regarding a young Wichita man who died and his body was found near. 137.

Newspapers in this era were well known for being sensationalistic, opportunistic, and not above breaking the law, or lying to get a story. Many papers were no doubt sold the day the new sellers called out "Jack the Ripper!" The story wove itself out that a certain Mrs. Jones who lived to the east of Oklahoma City, perhaps in one of the tent cities or small camps that dotted the river and the rails heading north and east toward Choctaw. The grass had grown tall and as she crossed the fields, a man suddenly sprang out and attacked her, slicing her throat and leaving her for dead.

Clutching her throat, blood streaming down the front of her, she stumbled out where others could find her. Pandemonium ensued as people scurried to get her help and to track down the dastardly attacker. 138

A lot of papers were probably sold that day, and new locks, and bullets for guns grown dusty from a quiet life in the 'big town.'

Earlier that year, Homer Wilkins' body was found by a night watchman near the Ridenour-Mercantile Company on East California in Oklahoma City. During the night a guard with the MKT had fired a shot at what he had supposed were prowlers. Police were inclined to think this was the shot that killed young Homer.139

1913

Young Donald Cloud, Ollie Berry and Henry Walters were struck at a crossing by a Midland Valley switch engine. Injuries for all were thought to fatal. The Engineer said he saw nothing of the boys when he backed out of the freight house.140

Rock Island Passenger Train No. 726 hit and killed two men, Will Hutchins, 29 and John Sanders, 18, west of Yukon. The men were "apparently sleeping." One of the victims, Hutchins, had a rocky past and had recently been pursued by motorcycle officers through "South Town and Capitol Hill."141

1914

While a couple of the incidents related in following years are clearly potential homicides disguised as accidents and some bald murders, the rate of incidents decreases. Greater emphasis on railroad safety, education of people about the dangers, and increased police presence no doubt contributed to the reduced numbers. Also, the rumblings of war in Europe may have caused attention to shift, whatever the cause, the number and the nature of the deaths near railways changed. There were other interesting events that emerged to cause one to wonder about patterns and connections.

Few recorded instances of missing children were found while surveying records. Some exceptions remain, the young immigrant girl who disappeared, a couple of children reported stolen by strangers, and Harry Priester. There were a couple of cases of incest reported to authorities and child beatings severe enough to warrant mention. So it was unique when the body of 9-year-old Ella Young was found in late 1912, or early 1913. Her small skull had been fractured by a blunt instrument and she was covered in blood. Her body was found near Kiefer close to Sapulpa in eastern Oklahoma. Reported missing, a large group had quickly searched for her with detectives and bloodhounds, but she was not located unto too late. A young man was questioned but no results achieved.142

Sometimes life is simply too much to handle and a person finds themselves afflicted by mental conditions or hopelessness. The final resort then seems logical and the answer to their problems. In truth, they simply leave their troubles with the ones they leave behind who must grieve and cope with their deep loss. In a lonely clearing, near a tree in March when the trees are still half denuded and barren, B.H. Hildebrand, formerly of Ft. Sill, was found near the Frisco depot, a .32 caliber pistol found nearby and a bullet hole in his temple. A neatly packed suitcase and .42 cents were all of his property found. A letter to a girl, Aggie Phillips, addressed but not mailed, in his suitcase gave circumstantial suggestion of suicide.143

The sprawling Oklahoma City area and was seeing increased traffic between the heart and the outlying communities along the "Interurban" rail system. Carelessness as well as the criminal element contributed to some of the accidents and deaths.144

This period is an official "hobo" or "tramp" time. Gentlemen of the road, wandering souls, or a hundred other labels described these men whose preferred a life style that was transitory. Some were veterans from the Spanish-American War who had not been able to integrate back into society. Some were ex-convicts who swore to never sleep under a roof again and longed for the wide skies. Among them were a few who wanted to disappear for a while and some who were con men and panhandlers. It has even been suggested the road was a pathway for men who lived an alternative lifestyle.

Most would follow the rail lines, using the rail section camps or abandoned "tent cities" once the workers had moved on. Some would find safe havens beneath bridges or trestles and others knew the warren of warehouses in the train yards of a dozen cities.

Many used a short hand or pictographic language that warned other men of the road of dangers or pointed them to places where a hot meal and warm, dry place to sleep might be found. One woman recalled how, as a small child, these hobos would come by their house (just off the rail line). They were courteous and well mannered. Curious the woman and her sister searched around and found a symbol on one corner of their property labeling their house a "friendly family; good cook."145

Propped up against a pile of ties an unknown man greeted the Rock Island section crews as they began their afternoon's work. Head hanging down to the collar of a rough overcoat, legs sprawled, half-eaten load of bread on the ground all seemed to point to sudden death. "The man seemed to have fallen asleep and died." Contents of the man's pockets included matches, a box-opening tool, two tin spoons, and a scrap of paper, torn from a checkbook, with the name

"F.T. Schaetzel." Nothing else found on the man helped lead to identification.146

In mid-year several crimes shocked eastern Oklahoma and had echoes of strange crimes elsewhere in the country. Like in the notorious unsolved murders of June 1912 in Villisca, Iowa, the weapon of choice was a convenient one, and one which would cause few heads to turn, an axe.[147] Merchants in the region of Muskogee, Charles Everitt and B.F. Richardson, had been killed earlier that year. In Braggs that fall, a hatchet fiend seemed at work. In that small town on the Missouri and Pacific track line, Anna Martin was attacked in her bed. Local merchant William Herzog were attacked and brutally assaulted by an axe welding man as he slept. Despite the use of the famed Pinkerton's and the local Burns agency detectives, no clues emerged.148

1915

The accounts begin to slow down due to unknown factors but suspicious deaths continue to occur. The powerful engines and long line of heavy cars continued to provide ample opportunity for a killer to cover their tracks. It also highlighted aspects of society and raises issues of the drug culture in early Oklahoma, the state of mental health care, and the alternatives of people to leave destructive relationships. All provide the framework for the motives that often drive people to act criminally and may contribute to understanding the real story of this macabre underbelly of Oklahoma history.

A local woman, known to Oklahoma City authorities as the wife of one "Dopey" or "Insect" Jones, was found dead after she stepped in front of a train. It was assumed she had been in the throes of a drug when she walked into the train. She was a picturesque character often seen wandering the streets, living in tents, and roaming the parks playing an accordion and taking donations.149 Her death was also a subtle reminder that the drug problem in Oklahoma, first noted as early as 1910, was still thriving. Antlers, Oklahoma saw also saw a telegraph clerk robbed and body placed on the tracks to hide the crime.150

A clear 'copycat' murder occurred in Muskogee in August in September as Mrs. Province was charged with the hatchet murder of her grocer husband. The deed, so reminiscent of murders just the year before in Muskogee and Braggs, was quickly laid at the feet of the sudden widow.151

1916

World War I was raging in Europe and many young men, and the not so young, found themselves in the trenches or training to go "over there." As a result, there were fewer noted deaths of the nature recorded before and after this year.

Did military service snatch up the travelers, the restless, and homeless into the war or associated work?

Does this infer that a killer or killers were themselves involved in the conflict? Were other locations riper for the particular skill of such a killer?

Are there other stories, hidden in forgotten and crumbling records, which shed light on the truth?

1917

Could a killer have been in a down cycle, injured, or simply trying new things during this period? Mysteries abound in the era – delightfully unsolved and unsolvable. News accounts were more pedestrian as well.

A woman, registered as "T. Brown, Tulsa" had committed suicide in the Grand Hotel and remained unknown. Her hat bore the name of a shop at Chickasha but no other clues were apparent and no cause of her death could be determined. She would most likely have arrived on a train and had quietly and invisibly taken her last room.152

1918

In February, however, there was another strange death that remains intriguing. An unidentified, forty year old man's body was found four miles northeast of the city on the farm of Ed Baker. According to the accounts, the man did the nearly impossible by committing suicide by cutting his own throat so severely the head had been nearly "severed from the body." The Coroner T.F. Donnell confidently declared, however, that it was a "clear case of suicide." The location was only about 50 yards from the "old street car line", that ran to the Northeast Lake. The victim was known to have worked for the farmer, Baker, but would not give his name.153

L.H. Beltzer, in the name of his son Clarence Beltzer, 14, claimed the youth had fallen asleep on the tracks near Chandler while in the company of another boy, Ralph Wright. He further claimed the engineer saw the boy and could have stopped but did not. The boy was struck by the train and injured, it was claimed but no statement explained why the boys did not move.154

The engineer of the inbound Norman electric car saw the body of the young man on the track, "as if asleep." He was unable to stop the car in time and the young man, around 26, was struck. Police surmised he might have been, because of his dress, a mechanic but were unable to determine anything else because there were no papers on the body.[155]

1919

Nine-year-old Ezra Thompson was sleeping on the tracks when Car No. 9 approached at great speed. Motorman Grove C. Brown, hurriedly slowed down and picked up the child to carry him to the next stop. [156]

Near Cement, Oklahoma two youths fell asleep on a curve. Morris Fox of Casper, WY, 15, claimed he had rolled out of the way of the train while still asleep. His companion, Viel Johnson of Lawton, however, was killed instantly under the wheels of the train.[157]

1920

From Wichita Falls, Texas, where the journey may have first begun back in the 1890's, a body was found. The 18-year-old KATY worker was discovered in a boxcar with a bloody club nearby. The man's body was found in Henryetta.

A warrant was issued for the train crew's Italian cook.158

An unknown man was found along the Santa Fe tracks several short pieces of blasting fuse by his body. Police said it looked from the damage to the body as if the man had ignited a stick of dynamite and then laid his head down on the charge. The only identifying item on his person was a pocket piece with a Yukon (Oklahoma) firm's name.159

ASLEEP ON THE TRACKS: A CLOSER LOOK

Frank woke in the cold dawn feeling a dozen sharp rocks stabbing him like miniature knives. He tried to sit up and tasted the rancid remains of the cheap whiskey he had had the night before. He had stupidly lost his money in a card game, decided to walk home, and was following the track so he would not wonder off into the night. His head felt like it was going split apart any minute and he struggled to prop himself up on the cold metal of the rail.

Dizzily the world spun around and he felt more than a little sick. He had to get up. Some sound had him groggily turning around and he realized he was too late. The heavy metal cowcatcher struck him flipping him upwards and then trapping him as it roared on its way. Screaming in agony he feels the wheel tear flesh and sever bones before he is kicked away to roll into the dew covered grass. The sun is just lifting over the trees as he breaths his last breath and his blood waters the weeds by the railroad tracks.

      One of the enduring questions related to some rail deaths is how does a person remains asleep as a loud, massive engine steams towards them and a train rumbling over iron and steel tracks that would have sent out a warning in the form of vibrations? The roar of the engine, the escape of steam in a shrill whistle should have heralded the approach. Explanations are not complementary and if based on more recent episodes probably involved drugs, drink, and suicide attempts. Some, however, were clearly something more.

"Dead Runaway Boys at Ardmore." The Oklahoman (Aug.12, 1925):9. Two young men, Clayton McCoy and Leo Arnett, inmates of the reform school at Paul's Valley had run away, and thought be returning, when they died near Paoli.

"Freight Car Sleeper Has Legs Cut Off." The Oklahoman (June 23, 1930):1. A probable "gentlemen of the road" (a term for a hobo) was asleep atop a car when it

was bumped by the switch engine. He was knocked off, it was believed, and run over on the Rock Island tracks. His only identification noted a possible brother, "Mike", in Salem, Ohio.

"City Man Reported Killed by Train." The Oklahoman (Aug.8, 1932): 1. From Lexington, MO came the news that a Clarence Sartin, 25, was thought to have fallen asleep on the tracks bear Henrietta. Although, thought to have come from the Oklahoma City area, none by that name had family named Clarence. Note: This intrigued me on a personal level because in my family tree there is the name "Sartin." The story my father told me was that the name was given to his father as a middle name because of neighbors in Barry County, Missouri, that were much admired.

"Youth Asleep on Rails, Prober Says." The Oklahoman (Sept. 4, 1935):4. After investigation by the county's "evidence man", the death of Robert Tyler, 17, had been due to the young man falling asleep on the interurban tracks near Britton in Oklahoma County.

"Man Killed As He Dozes On Railraod." The Oklahoman (July 2, 1936): 13. Near Okmulgee, J.B. Wynn, 23 and Bob Francher, were involved in an auto-train incident involving 'falling asleep'. The pair had stopped their auto and both were resting, Wynn with his head near the tracks, when the incident occurred.

"Three Men Killed By Kansas Train." The Oklahoman (Aug.27, 1936):9. Near Mildred, Kansas three unidentified men were killed and parts of their bodies "strewn for miles". The incident occurred near no crossing causing the Sheriff to suggest they had fallen asleep. Although not in Oklahoma, it shows the continuing trend of falling asleep on the tracks was still around at this late date.

"City Man Killed When Struck By Rock Island Engine." The Oklahoman (July 29, 1941): 1. Just why 31 year-old Pat Rogers, who lived within a mile of the switchyards, would have fallen asleep on the tracks was not addressed in the article. When first witnessed on the tracks people thought he was merely asleep, but the crews were unable to halt the train or remove him in time.

"Train Kills Boys Escaping School." The Oklahoman. (July 25, 1941):1. "Two believed asleep on tracks near Davis". The two 15-year-olds, George Knight and Jimmy Coppage, were at the state training school near Paul's Valley when the event occurred.

"Bodies of Two Youths Found on Railway Tracks." The Oklahoman (Sept.17, 1942):12. It was assumed that the bodies of Leroy Chuculate, 15 and George Williams, 18, both of Bunch, Oklahoma, had died because they had fallen asleep. The 'mangled bodies' had been found on the

KC Southern RR tracks near Bunch where they had been run over during the night after going to a nearby dance.

"Body, Asleep by Track, Killed." The Oklahoman (Sept.4, 1942): 5. Maxie J. Cheetham, 17 of Alabama was killed sleeping beside a railroad track near Dallas. A companion said they were" riding freight trains to California."

PHYSICAL ENVIRONMENT

A photographer specializing in filming freight trains complained of the intense vibrations as the train approached and sought advice on how stabilize the camera to avoid the blurring.160
    In the film, "Coal Miner's Daughter", there is a scene were young Loretta Lynn is at the depot with her father. Down the narrow hollow comes a huge steam locomotive belching black billows of smoke, hissing steam, whistle blowing, wheels chugging, and ground shaking. The actors have to raise their voices over the approaching engine.161   In that scene the space is quite similar to the distances described in many of these stories of people said to have fallen asleep on the tracks in Oklahoma.

Modern technology of better rails, engines, wheels, and power have improved rail travel from those black locomotives of the past. State and federal regulations control issues of noise pollution, safety, and operation. Even with all of these improvements, the trains that cross the land today are still loud and powerful. They are a force not to be reckoned with lightly.

The trains of 1900 were loud, powerful, and rougher. They were a bucking bronco of the industrial revolution and only slowly tamed. Common weights for the engine and tender alone could be close to 500 tons.[162] Speeds of 100 mph were not impossible but probably not common.[163] In the Oklahoma stories, speed may have been an issue but not to that degree. Only once was there a major comment on speed, the train was going upwards of fifty miles an hour, yet at another accident scene the speed was said to be only twelve.

The trains produced ground vibrations. Studies exist for the environmental impact of ground vibrations for constructing various buildings and the levels of vibrations tolerated. Few clearly address the issue as related to older locomotives, but newer studies may serve as starting point. The transit of the multi-ton train over the tracks generates vibrations transmit through the tracks but also into the adjacent soil and/or rock substrata with the result the train is "felt."164

The trains of that era were loud. Between the whistles, the engines and the clatter they were not stealthy. In fact, the 'Doppler Effect" originated in hearing the passing of a train's whistle. Experts in auditory studies indicate that the modern train whistle registers 90 decibels (dB) at 500 feet distance.165 The average alarm clock categorized as "very loud", for comparison, registers only 80 dB.166 A study from New Mexico indicated their new 'Rail Runner', constructed to be quieter and EPA friendly, had station noise levels of 50 to 70 decibels, its whistle would affect at a distance of 1600 feet, and the train running at a constant 35 mph would have short bursts of 70-80 dB.167 These are all modern trains and logically the early trains were louder.

Perhaps one of the strangest questions in this strange issue is why does this still happen? Two Maine teen girls in 2008 decided to walk home from a party, fell asleep in the middle of the track and woke up only in time to roll most of their bodies off the tail. One girl lost a left and the other a foot. The girls admitted to being "wicked tired" and normally heavy sleepers.168 In 2006, a London man fell asleep in the middle of the tracks and narrowly missed death as trains were diverted in the nick of time and the man was finally arrested for being drunk and disorderly (despite being asleep).169

PART 5:
WHERE THE RAIL GOES

One striking feature of many of these tales of "gruesome death" is the way they often follow, sequentially, the spider web of the rails. From January to December, deaths were traced along various train routes in deadly progressions. The deaths that had common features seem to fall along the rail lines in specific geographical regions.

Regional Locations:

Northwest Oklahoma: *Enid, Kingfisher, El Reno, Yukon*

Central & OKC: *Oklahoma City, Capitol Hill, Bethany, Norman, Noble, Edmund*

Northeast Oklahoma: *Wagoner, Muskogee, Sallisaw, Tulsa, Keystone, Bristow, Shawnee, Pawnee*

Southeast Oklahoma: *Atoka, Ardmore, Davis*

Southwest Oklahoma: *Frederick, Chickasha, Lawton, Duncan*

Trans Regional Locations:

Deaths can be trailed moving between regional rail lines, apparently skipping to other carriers with some possible patterns emerging involving the railways involved. Further research might indicate even clearer patterns emerging for both Oklahoma and nearby states.

Date	Place/Region	Railway line
1901, October	Anadarko	Rock Island
1901, November	Wellston	Frisco
1901, November	Shawnee	Choctaw
1902, April	Wagoner	
1902, August	Shawnee	Choctaw
1902, October	Noble	
1903, July	Edmond	Santa Fe
1903, December	Shawnee	Choctaw
1904, January	OKC	Choctaw/Frisco
1904, March	Kingfisher	
1904, April	Shawnee	Choctaw
1904, April	OKC	Frisco
1904, April	Frederick	MT&K
1904, November	Chickasha	Rhode Island
1904, December	Jones	St. Louis/SanFran/MT&K
1904, December	Fletcher	
1904, December	OKC	
1905, January	Coretta (Wagoner Co.)	
1905, February	Summit	
1905, March	OKC	
1905, June	OKC	KATY
1905, September	OKC	KATY
1905, November	Bartlesville	
1905, November	OKC	
1905, November	OKC	
1906, January	OKC	
1906, April	Tulsa	
1906, May	Davis	

When Death Rode the Rails

1906, June	OKC	Santa Fe
1906, July	Tulsa	Frisco
1906, July	Noble	
1906, July	Bristow	Frisco
1906, August	Cache	Frisco
1906, August	OKC	Rhode Island
1906, October	Lawton	Rhode Island
1906, October	Amarillo, TX (OK Victim)	
1907, January	Harrah	Rhode Island
1907, January	Chickasha	Rhode Island
1907, February	OKC	
1907, February	OKC	
1907, February	Dewey	
1907, February	Henryetta	Frisco
1907, March	Iowa (Ok Victim)	
1907, April	Lawton	
1907, May	Pawnee	
1907, June	OKC	
1907, June	OKC	Santa Fe
1907, June	Norman	
1907, July	Yarnby	
1907, July	Atoka	
1907, July	Chickasha	Frisco
1907, August	Dawson	
1907, August	Shawnee	
1907, September	Yukon/El Reno	
1907, September	Frederick	
1907, October	Enid	Frisco
1907, December	Shawnee	
1907, December	McAlester	
1908, January	OKC	
1908, April	Wynnewood	Santa Fe
1908, April	Rush Springs	
1908, June	Holdenville	Frisco / Santa Fe
1908, July	OKC	Frisco
1908, August	Nowata	Iron Mountain
1908, December	OKC	Santa Fe
1908, December	Tulsa	
1908, December	OKC	Santa Fe
1908, December	Deep Fork	

	(OKC)	
1909, January	Tulsa	Frisco
1909, January	Muskogee	KATY
1909, January	OKC (Capitol Hill)	Santa Fe
1909, February	Chickasha	
1909, March	Muskogee	
1909, April	Chickasha	
1909, May	McAlester	
1909, August	OKC	
1909, August	Chickasha	Rhode Island
1909, August	Tulsa	KATY
1909, October	Panama	
1909, October	Muskogee	
1909, October	Davis	
1909, November	Sapulpa	
1910, January	OKC	
1910, February	Bonner Springs, KS (OK Victim)	
1910, June	Chickasha	
1910, August	OKC	
1910, November	Tulsa	Frisco
1910, December	OKC	Frisco
1911, January	OKC	Frisco
1911, February	Tulsa	
1911, July	Weleetka	
1911, November	McAlester	
1912, August	Renfrow	
1912, August	OKC	
1913, May	Midland Valley	
1913, September	Yukon	Rhode Island
1914, January	Kiefer	
1914, March	Chickasha	Frisco
1914, June	Needham	
1914, October	OKC	Rhode Island

PART 6:
SUSPECTS & SUSPICIONS

Where earlier officials had a tendency to cry accident whenever they found bodies found on, or near, the tracks, by statehood many officials clearly had suspicions about those victims found on the tracks or near them. The deaths were more often determined by a coroner or an inquest jury and less by the officers finding the body.

Knowing that, hints that those in the time had more than a few suspicions about many of these deaths and helps solidify the theory of a killer(s) at work. One has to ask then, if a serial killer (or killers) roamed early day Oklahoma who might that person or persons have been?

Several facts present themselves in attempting to "profile" a serial killer. In the days of Jack-the-Ripper, there was little known difference between the "mad" and the "bad." Times change, for good and ill, and modern law enforcement recognizes that these killers fall into several categories. They may not be totally united in accepting the specific process or chronology required creating a serial killer, but they recognize these killers tend to come in different types.

As to causes, some psychologists argue that certain people are born with their emotional wiring capable of short-circuiting in a deadly manner. Others tend to believe that such killers emerge from some early and long-term trauma or abuse in their own lives. While still others suggest through a combination of several factors including brain damage, early trauma or abuse, and some triggering event, such killers are created.

It is safe to postulate several facts. He had to have been male because to have been female in that environment would have raised comment. Although numerous women successfully masqueraded as men in the 19th and 20th century, it was usually for reasons of personal freedom or to hide from a situation, and they were possibly rare. In addition, researches into modern random and violent serial killers shows a predominance of them are male. Plus, he would have had to have some relationship or even skill with the railroads so that his presence would not raise alarm or concern. He could have been a "tramp" who regularly rode the trains illegally, but he could have also been a brakeman, a switchman, an engineer, a hired guard, a supplier, a member of a rail repair crew, a wrecking crew, or an employee of one of the service centers.

As the coal and oil industries boomed, railroad spurs connected those service sites to the major lines increasing access and opportunity for a wider pool of people. In addition, the work force of the crews and support centers was often itinerant and varied almost daily making it no doubt difficult to know everyone.

Tramps, later commonly known as "hobos," are common to periods of economic upheaval and after wars, or military actions. The 1880-1890's saw a depression sweep the country, banks wobbled, and railroads gobbled up small farm holdings in the name of imminent domain. The youngest veterans of the Civil War were still just reaching their later years, but younger men rode with Teddy Roosevelt and his Rough Riders in San Juan, and numerous other men were veterans of campaigns in the west against native warriors and criminal renegades. Some of the men who took to the road were also men living an alternative lifestyle and their homosexuality in that time made transitory movement a necessity.170

    If the early deaths in northern Texas join the mix, and those found bear a striking similarity (as well as important links to rail lines going into Oklahoma), the killer could have been in his thirties in the 1890's. If he continued killing over the next thirty years (to about 1925) he would only be in or nearing his sixties. Experts indicate 'cooling off' periods and migration are also not unusual. Other research into these types of killings, indicate there may have been other violent incidences in his life earlier. The harsh work of the early rail lines, into the still wild and wooly west of the 1890's, would have provided the right atmosphere and opportunity for someone with a growing taste for violence.

Lone Man Traveling the Railroad Theory: This theory suggests that a man with serial killing tendencies may have been at work in northern Texas in the 1890's working the Missouri, Kansas, & Texas rail line. This line entered the eastern part of Oklahoma (then known as the Indian Territory) very early and by statehood had a long history in the region. Some of the earliest stories are about bodies discovered near Wagoner in the Tulsa area as the rail lines expanded, new bodies are discovered along those M.T.& K lines as well.

Railroad Gang Hired to Cause Trouble Theory: The competition was fierce in Oklahoma among numerous regional rail companies and the larger corporations. Several small companies were absorbed into the larger and more expanding lines: Rock Island, San Francisco, Pacific, St. Louis, and others. Thus, smaller regional lines like the "Choctaw" and "Gulf" would soon disappear. Some railroads, like other industries, attracted men who sought power and influence by any means available. If a company were indecisive about an offer from another line, maybe a little nudge would settle the issue. Some stories of thefts, accidents, attacks, and wrecks might be attributed to just this type of influence.

Criminals Using the Crimes to Cover Their Tracks Theory: In 1907, as Oklahoma became a state, there was already a well organized criminal element in the state supplying many of the needs of criminals. Illegal gambling, liquor, prostitution, counterfeiting, and confidence games were almost daily events in Oklahoma City and the surrounding regions. Keeping their plans confidential, eliminating threats, and insuring cooperation may account for beatings, masquerades as police officers, 'suicides', and other crimes located around various rail hubs, lines, or yards. In this same general category one can place political groups, anti or pro socialists, racists, thieves, and murderers. All of these and more were at work in the state and may have employed similar tactics.

Copycat Killing Using Railroad to Cover Crime Theory: As early as the 1890's, newspapers carried tales of murderers who attempted to hide their crime by placing the victim on a nearby train track. Someone caught in the wake of a rash act of violence may have remembered hearing or reading such a story might have been given ideas leading to 'copycat' killings.

Having a train depot was a sign of economic viability for small communities and many aggressively sought out the right to be a train town. Little things like murder in a community tend to deflate the booster pride just a little and drive away prospective investors. So if such tales were swept under the communal carpet to be lost over time, it is not too surprising.

PART 7:
THE VICTIMS

Looking across the broad range of victims involved in these cases, several things become apparent. These suspect cases involve only a few women, but many young men, several children or teens, and several older men. What these all have in common is that they would be possibly easy targets.

The nature of the hunting grounds could have dictated the sex of the victims as few women were involved in working or traveling the freight lines. A preferred demographic of males would have also have attracted the killer to such an environment. For a mature man, moreover, younger men (12-24) could be easy to approach with offers of jobs, money, or illicit activities. Children and older men could both be just as easily overpowered.

Young Children

Few young children are mentioned in the Oklahoma accounts if bodies of infants buried in cans, shallow graves, and similar situations are accepted at face value. Poverty stricken workers, homeless members of traveling railroad camps, sometimes had family with them and stillbirths, illness, and accidents occurred and burial out in the wide open spaces was a given. Occasionally, horrific tales of infants tossed off of trains cropped up in regional newspapers. All carried the patina of urban legend with an echo of a real event. It was the assumed the incident involved a 'wronged girl,' distraught, seeking to rid herself of the social shame of a child born outside of marriage. A few occasions did see shocking crimes occur involving children: a young girl who went missing, a young boy murdered, and a young child reporting incest in the home of a community leader. These few occasions hint that undercurrents existed in the society of the "good old days" to equal modern social ills.

Teens to Young Adult

Many of the most puzzling deaths involved young men of a similar age range. On the one hand it would not be surprising that this age group might die in greater numbers. They were young, mobile, apparently orphaned or runaways who lacked the familial or social training that helps prevent accidents. Thus they assumed a high-risk life style by launching out on their own and traveling along potentially dangerous routes. Many of the victims in this age group were also, and sadly, described as "unknown."

Middle Aged

Most of the deaths for men from 27-50 were the accidents, workers misjudging as they tried to move to a train, workers who fell walking the roof of the cars, or men who committed clear suicides.

Elderly

Another large group of deaths occurred in men above 57 years of age. They were another easy prey for human predators. They were often found by railroad tracks apparently 'hit by trains', dead by assumed suicides, and sometimes found beaten to a pulp for the few goods they possessed.

Sex

Males were the usual victim and only a few instances of a female killed by a train could be found comparable to the other deaths. Most of the women who suicide preferred poisons or guns to do the deed. Most of the women involved in rail deaths appeared to be accidents caused by miss-steps, falls, or too casual a contact with the trains.

THE DEATHS

This chart lists the deaths initially identified as suspicious due to their location, mode of death, connection to railroads, or similar rationale.

The outcome of some deaths could not be determined as no follow-up article was found; no records (death, cemetery, news articles) could verify final determination. The "?" indicate room for some doubt exists for an accidental death when considered within the larger context of events.

Date	Place	Victim(s) Spellings as listed in news accounts	Age	Death Ruled Murder (M); Sleeping (S); Suicide (SU); Accident (A), Unknown (U)
1901	Anadarko	John Tilley		M
1901	Wellston	John Bushman		S
1901	Shawnee	UNK	35	M
1902	Wagoner	Will Haynes	25	M
1902	Blackwell	Combs Family poisoned		Lived
1902	Shawnee	J.L. Hodges	54	M
1902	Noble	Joe Ragel, Hugh	15	S

When Death Rode the Rails

		Morrow, Daniel Carnahan		
1903	Cleveland	Olive Rayl		SU
1903	Shawnee	UNK		M
1903	Edmond	John Williams	13	A
1904	E. OKC	UNK/"G.K."	35	A?
1904	Kingfisher	John G. Miller	40	M
1904	Shawnee	Willie McDaniel	Ca.40	?
1904	Frederick	UNK – Skeleton/shallow grave	?	?
1904	OKC	Willie Duncan, fire	12	A?
1904	El Reno	James H. Squires		A
1904	Chickasha	G.A. Richards, J.F. Johnston		A?
1904	Jones City	W.A. Agee	60	M
1904	Fletcher	Nona Smith	14	UNK/disappeared
1904	OKC	Wm. R. Dunn	54	M
1904	Shawnee	Rail man attempted to cut passenger		
1904	Muskogee	UNK	Mid-aged	M
1904	Wellston	Brunzy Gayhowski	11	UNK/Disappeared
1905	Coretta	UNK	22	A
1905	Muskogee	Charles E. Spencer; J.E. Martin		A
1905	OKC	W. Menze, attacked		
1905	OKC	Joe Churchwell, attacked		
1905	OKC	P.Charbeneau		M?
1906	Lawton	G.H. Pollock, IA	74	M
1906	NM	Rev. Hillhouse, Bartlesville	75	?
1906	OKC	John Robinson		M
1906	Tulsa	UNK		M
1906	Davis	UNK	Infant	UNK
1906	Lawton	J.K. Thompson	Ca.40	A?/drowned in 2 inches of water
1906	OKC	UNK	15	A?/falling logs

When Death Rode the Rails   145

1906	Tulsa	Harry Priester	8	M
1906	OKC	UNK	15	A?
1906	Bristow	Harry Brown, J. Reynolds, George Reynolds	15,12, 27	A?
1906	Lawton	G.H. Pollock, IA	74	M
1906	OKC	Arthur Reynolds	56	A
1906	Amarillo,TX	Earl Dockery of Ok	14-25	M
1906	OKC	UNK	Infant	U
1907	Harrah	H. Hogan	51	A
1907	Chickasha	Mike Meany, rail road worker, charged with trying to cut throat of J.V. Wegelenak		
1907	OKC	UNK "tramp"	23	U
1907	Shawnee	Paul Randall	20	A?
1907	Henryetta	J. Aubry		M
1907	Sioux City, IA	Bert McFadden of Enid		M
1907	Pawnee	Roy Hadley disappeared with tall man	12	U
1907	Chickasha	UNK, with Swedish badge, crushed by logs with arms crossed	14	A?
1907	Flynn (OKC)	R.A. Rowe		M
1907	Lawton	UNK/missing ears		M
1907	OKC	Wilber Gunreith		M
1907	Dawson	UNK	76	M
1907	Ardmore	Seth Hazle		A?
1907	Durant	UNK	25	M
1907	Enid	C.L. Cardwell		M
1907	Capitol Hill	S.P. Adams		A
1907	McAlester	A. J. Ruyle		M
1908	OKC	UNK		A
1908	El Reno	John Sparks	50s	M
1908	Wynnewood	UNK/bloody mattress by tracks		M

1908	Chickasha	Charles Cooper		M
1908	Muskogee	UNK		A?
1908	OKC	T.R. Weems		A?
1908	Alva	Jack Davis		A
1908	OKC	Missing teen	18	U
1908	Tulsa	Wm Smith/throat cut		M
1908	OKC	UNK		A
1908	Stigler	Thomas Baker		A
1908	OKC	UNK	Middle age	M
1908	OKC	John Nitzel		SU/hanging
1908	OKC, North.	C.A. Appln		A
1908	McAlester	"Night riders" Intimidating		
1909	Keystone	UNK/D.B. Achley?		M
1909	Mulhall	Cora E. Murrell, Station Agent bound & gagged	18	
1909	Capital Hill	Johnnie Cloutte, bound & gagged for 24 hours	13	
1909	Muskogee	UNK/ throat cut		M
1909	McAlester	Guy Roe	13	A?
1909	OKC	Dee Brooks		M
1909	Chickasha	UNK	"boy"	A?
1909	Tulsa	O.M. Herford		A
1909	Chickasha	UNK/ A. R. Synder	21	M?
1909	Muskogee	I. Gray		Su?
1909	Sapulpa	Mrs. David Croy/ attacked/throat cut		?
1909	Muskogee	Charles Blade		M
1910	Kansas	Earl Gregory, Guthrie	20	A?
1910	OKC	J.H. Lem	74	M
1910	Enid	UNK	18	Natural?
1910	Edmond	Thomas C. Hill, attacked, left for dead		
1910	Chickasha	W.J. Russell	Elderly	A
1910	Davis	Claud Johnson		M

1912	Nowata	Irene Goheen		M
1913	Tulsa	Donald Cloud, Ollie Berry, Henry Walters	10, 10, 10	A
1913	OKC	Eugene Osborne	16	A
1914	Bethany	Christina Manourek /poisoned but no bottle found/body in grass	25	Su?/M?
1914	Sapulpa	Ella Young	9	M
1914	Chickasha	B.H. Hillebrand	20's	Su
1917	OKC	T. Brown		A /Su
1914	OKC	UNK	28	U/A
1918	OKC	UNK	40	M/Su
1920	Henryetta	D.E. Stinton	18	M
1920	Ardmore	UNK/found w dynamite		UNK
1921	OKC	G.V. Dodge		M
1932	Cleveland	Alvie Brown	32	A
1935	Madill	William Pratt	37	A

PART 8:
ENTER THE LAW MEN

An easy answer to these bodies found was that they had been "hit", "run over" or had "fallen asleep" on the tracks. Only so many of each can happen naturally. So who might be the culprit or culprits? An itinerant rail crew worker, hired thugs of the railroad, or some killer working the rail lines for victims and disposal of the bodies.

Around 1905-1910 there was an increase in attempted robberies, thefts of luggage, confidence tricks involving rail passes, and attempts to wreck trains. Newspaper accounts began mentioning "special agents" brought in by the railroad and local detectives (police and private) became more notable.

It can be inferred, from newspaper accounts that the total railroad situation became so dire that help was at work and maybe behind the scenes. Strangely, after statehood there is a sharp decrease in the number and frequency of deaths. What happened? Did daring special agents of the railroads, local constables, and private detectives use their combined efforts to put a dent in the crime rate? Did they in true "old west" style simply catch their man?

Did the unknown killer, however, simply get away to move into new regions? If records from nearby states were examined, would we find that the hunter had left for farther, and safer, fields to reap his harvest of mayhem?

The railroads had long operated a security force and they often appear to have traveled incognito with no names mentioned in some of the news stories. Most notable were the "Special Agents of the Railroad" who were fashioned after the U.S. Marshals. Some however, were simply station agents who also did "detective" work in locating lost luggage and stolen freight cars.

There was also a lot of competiveness among officers, detectives, and other investigators. Henry Burns, writing in the Oklahoman of 1910 noted the competition present in "Railroad Detective's Job is Easy: He Lets Police Do the Work" (Aug. 21, 1910:pg. 44). From early news stories in the Oklahoman, a few names do surface as Special Agents of the Railroads. Early days of Oklahoma City also saw a boom in "detective agencies" as ex-police, U.S. Marshalls, and others tried their hand at sleuthing.

Several people along the way fancied themselves a detective. Such as one young fellow who sleuthed his way down back alleys with a gun and a lantern. He crept around so he caught the eye of a local constable and ended up before a judge. The daughter of one local lawman even provided some service as a detective catching thieves in the act in a local department store.

PART 9:
SERIAL KILLERS

Well into the 20th century the term mass murderer (predecessor to today's serial killer) would have brought to mind a hulking caricature faced man ala an early anarchist drawing: ugly, deformed, creeping, stealth like, knife dripping blood and his evil intentions on clear display.

The serial killer came to level of popular knowledge in 1888 in foggy streets of London. Serial killers had existed prior to this, but were largely unrecognized until the cluster of murders in a poor district of London.

They might, like the pre-Civil War Harps of Kentucky or the Benders of Kansas (1870's) simply wait for their victims to come to them or traveled widely to hide their activities.

Whichever the case, the early 20th century saw several others achieve some notoriety: England's Dr. Harvey Crippen (1905-1910), the Thames Torso Murders of 1887-1902, H.H. Holmes and his infamous 1893 Chicago "Murder House" (who is considered by some as the first U.S. serial killer), and numerous other events all featured in national news and were spread by traveling guests.

Modern science and police work has learned a lot about serial killers in the last century. The FBI, the National Institute of Justice, and others have identified several characteristics related to how they function and operate. Psychologists and behaviorists have studied and interviewed such killers to learn triggers, motivations, methods, and conduct.

They have learned that most serial killers begin at an early age, they often have preferred victim "types," and they often use or prefer a specific killing method, but can be varied. They can be proficient in "fitting in" and keeping a low profile becoming the least likely suspect.171

Recently, concern arose over high levels of minerals and impurities in products and food being imported from China highlighted the need for standards of content, manufacture and product. This was something that threatened the United States in the late 1880's and brought about a revolution that produced the Food and Drug Administration.

Some experts suggest serial murder is "generational' and influenced by such things as child abuse, drug use, injury, malnutrition and heavy drinking.172

In the 1880's various medicines were available without prescriptions containing a variety of toxic elements, additives to food products would eventually create the 'pure food' crisis, and alcohol was abundant but uncontrolled as to content. Could these have influenced behaviors to the point that people became killers?

The famous "Jack the Ripper" appears in the last twenty years of the 19th century.173 Viewed often as an anomaly, but could he have been a precursor instead? Could the unexplained spike in homicides in 1905, be attributed to the blooming of seeds planted decades before in food, paint, water pipes, or medicines?

In all of these rail related deaths, bodies revealed a large number of "cut throats", "bashed heads", and "beaten bodies." These were all wounds that could be confused with damage from a train accident. The early competition between railroads may have meant hired 'muscle' may have been welcomed to put pressure on another line, to create havoc, and to clearly threaten.

This may have been a window of opportunity for someone to develop, or utilize, a proclivity for killing.

Several of the dead included young men who would have been easy targets since they were alone, vulnerable, and sometimes immigrants. As one case suggests, the victims may have been held prisoner and the fact that several skeletons are discovered in areas were other bodies were found may point to the route of the killer.

Recent evidence from killers in Asia, who operated much like the railroad killer of the United States, Angel Maturino Resendez, all suggests that such murderers can effectively utilize improved mobility as a means of killing across vast areas.174

The Axe Man Cometh

In fact, murderer Resendez himself may have been simply repeating a pattern of criminal activity dating far back into the early 20th century, and perhaps even earlier.

Across the American landscape, there was a time when every home had one staple tool used to chop wood, kill a rooster for Sunday dinner, or several other tasks. The axe was so useful and used by every member of a household: men, women, and even children. That such an instrument might be used in murders was not a surprise - murders often use what is handy, weapons of opportunity, or convenience.

Husbands went after wives and wives attacked husbands with an emphasis on single victim attacks. In some cases youth went after parental figures. Sometimes, a stranger came to town and struck in the shadows of night leaving blood and tragedy behind them before leaving once more.

The Crimes

What is more noticeable was that between 1909 and 1919 there were numerous axe murders of families or groups. These occurred across the country. Some were solved, some were merely officially closed by finding a local scapegoat, whole some remain a mystery to this day. To further confuse the issue an ax could be welded as easily by a woman or youth as a grown man. All were family units, killed in their sleep, with a blunt object such as a hammer, axe, pick, etc. or a sharp object such as an axe or a knife.

Although these could all be unrelated, except as copycat style crimes, the possibility remains that there could have been more crimes of a serial nature going in early 20th century America than previously supposed. They also share a common thread of being accessible by a close rail line.

If all these incidences were the work of one killer, the person obviously had issues with families and families where there was some potential, or perceived, problem as seen in the number of wives living apart from husbands, mothers living apart from fathers, etc. The killer may have seen, even in healthy families, some dysfunction he had to eradicate. He may have even seen himself as fulfilling some mission.

In at least two cases, there is the hint that it was the woman who was the recipient of the most severe attack supporting the theory the killer may have been substituting someone else for his victim. Was he lashing out at a substitute for some woman in his life? Was he killing the children to 'protect' them in some perverted reasoning?

Note, that many of these just might be the work of one man. A serial killer might go one for decades, uncaught, as has been proved many times over around the globe. The crime scenes were so contaminated by sight seers and investigators that valuable clues linking a perpetrator were lost almost before the story hit the news wire. Given that investigators even knew what to look for as evidence.

It would be interesting to determine how many of these cases saw the woman as the primary, or first, victim? How many had items thrown over clocks, telephones, and windows? How many left notes or had letters sent to the town reciting scriptures? These may all be the signature calling cards of the person responsible for these ghastly murders.

- In November of 1901, the Wilcox family of Los Angeles was 'knifed horribly' while they

slept. ("Horrible Crime", Oklahoman, Nov. 29, 1901, pg. 1).
- In Nov. 1904 an entire family was shot and the house burned in Auburn, Ca (Oklahoman, Nov. 12, 1904, pg. 1).
- In March 1905, San Rafael, CA a man "Murdered His Entire Family", Oklahoman, May 25, 105, pg. 7).
- In October 1909, James McMahon confessed to killing the Van Royen family in Kansas City. ("I Killed Them" Yells Murderer", Oklahoman, Oct. 27, 1909, pg.11).
- In November of 1909 in Bluebird, W. Va. a family was killed and the house burned down to try to cover the deed. ("Charred Bodies of Four found in Ruins of House." Oklahoman, Nov.2, 1909, pg. 10).
- December 1909, Cleveland, OH woman Josephine Mangero and her two children fatally stabbed. ("Mother and two children Slain". Oklahoman, Dec.5, 1909, pg. 1.).
- In 1909-1911, the New Orleans and Teas areas saw the murders of numerous families. It was assumed a sacrificial cult or sect was responsible and one young woman 'confessed' to such ("How the Cruel and Gruesome Murder of Africa's Serpent Worship Have Been revived in Louisiana," Oklahoman, Feb.18, 1912, pg. 38). Such stories were often printed to stir things up among the fearful whites and to create environments where mob

rule could function without too much complaint. The scope of these stories, despite the attempts to marginalize the killings as a racial issue, indicates a killer was prowling the area and using the rails to move about.

- In December 1910, Savannah, Georgia a race war almost ensued after the deaths of Mrs. Elizabeth Gribble, Mrs. Carrie Ohlander, and Mrs. Maggie Hunter. The local police rounded up over a hundred local African Americans to be 'questioned'. ("Woman Slain by Fiendish Negro." Oklahoman, Dec.12, 1909, pg. 18).
- In January 1911, Rayne, LA a mother and her four children were killed.+
- In Spring 1911, Lafayette, LA the Norbett Randall family was killed.+
- In September 1911, Colorado Springs, Co. People in several neighboring houses were discovered dead with crushed heads while they slept. Victims were an H.C.Wayne, his wife and child; a Mrs. A. J. Burnham, two children (including a one year old).*
- In October 1911, in Monmouth, IL a William E. Dawson, his wife, and daughter were killed.
- In October 1911, in Ellsworth, Kansas a William Showman, wife, and three children were killed as they slept.* ("Showman Family of Five Murdered." Ellsworth Reporter, Oct.11, 1911).
- In 1912, Crowly, LA a family was killed as they slept. + (+/ = Some assume these LA

and TX murders to be racially motivated as they are all African-American family units. Some included 'Mulatto' or mixed race children which further complicates and confuses the matter. The simple truth might also be that these families were convenient kills providing a prey separated from the major part of the society by racial prejudice and thus making them targets of ease. Others suggest some obscure church of sacrifice was involved yet the evidence appears weak to non-existent for this line of reasoning.)

- In 1912, Lake Charles, LA, a family was killed as they slept. +
- In April 1912, San Antonio (Police suspected the man was using the Southern Pacific Railroad since November 1911. It was suggested if the theory of the killer using the rails was correct he would next hit there and he did).
- In February, 1912, in Beaumont, Texas a family was killed. +
- In June 1912, in Paola, Kansas a Rollin Hudson and wife were murdered. ("Murder Came in the Night", Western Spirit, June 14, 1912).
- In June 1912, in Vilasca, Iowa, eight were murdered as they slept. Victims: J.B. Moore and wife, four children, and two local girls, guests of his children.* ("Recent Ax Murders", Oklahoman, July, 14, 1912, pg. 1).

- In December 1912, two women were killed in Columbia, Missouri. ("Horrible Murder Committed", Columbia Herald, Dec.20, 1912).
- In 1913, in Muskogee, Oklahoma several lone people were murdered by an axe welding killer ("Second Hatchet Murder Mystery Stirs Muskogee", Oklahoman, Nov. 29, 1913, pg. 1).
- In July 6, 1914, Blue Island (Chicago), IL a family was butchered as they slept. Victims: Jacob Neslesla, wife, daughter, and an infant grandchild.* ("Axe of Assassin Deals Death to Sleeping Family," Oklahoman, July 7, 1914.)
- In 1919, New Orleans, more axe murders thought to be the work of gangs but also as likely a serial killer. Perhaps even the same killer?
- In 1920 in Turtle Lake, N.D. eight are killed on the Jacob Wolf farm. ("Police Seek Clues in Dakota Murder", Oklahoman, April 25, pg. 2, and April 26, 1920, pg. 33).
- In January of 1922, a mother and son are killed in Chicago. (Oklahoman, Jan. 23, 1922, pg.12.)
- In November 1928, Omaha was stricken by a 'hatchet slayer' kills three. (Oklahoman, Nov. 21, 1928).

As the Texas and Louisiana authorities noted, the killer(s) were never far from a railroad line in all of these murders. In fact, in several cases the trail died at a rail line, clearly indicating a killer might have hopped a train to escape. [175]

It should be remembered that all we know about serial killers and their conduct, motives, and methods is fairly recently learned. What was said to be ironclad just 10 years ago is already being tweaked based on new research. Research shows then that the hard and fast "rules" of criminal profiling have been extremely useful but they have to also be subject to revisions.

WHEN DEATH RODE THE RAILS

Several possibilities present us with rationale and logical reasons for the many accidents and deaths. They range from pure imagination to serious probability of crime. As the only detectives of ice cold crime scenes, any ideas offered may only be as viable as the best guesses of a Sherlock Holmes tale. What answers are most logical, reasonable, and best fits the total body of evidence?

Through fictionalized writing based on true events and practices some possible scenarios introduced the possibilities of what transpired across the rails of early day Oklahoma and elsewhere. These all happened or were thought to happen. Were the strange deaths merely a confluence of coincidence in a wild time of lawlessness? Were the more deadly individuals portrayed in the scenarios combined into one creature that preyed on others up and down the countryside?

Were they all merely an accident of the meeting of deadly machinery, careless or untrained people, and slow news?

Frank, who, woke in the cold dawn feeling a dozen sharp rocks stabbing him like miniature knives. He tried to sit up and tasted the rancid remains of the cheap whiskey he had had the night before. He had stupidly lost his money in a card game, decided to walk home, and was following the track so he would not wonder off into the night. His head felt like it was going split apart any minute and he struggled to prop himself up on the cold metal of the rail.

Dizzily the world spun around and he felt more than a little sick. He had to get up. Some sound had him groggily turning around and he realized he was too late. The heavy metal cowcatcher struck him flipping him upwards and then trapping him as it roared on its way. Screaming in agony he feels the wheel tear flesh and sever bones before he is kicked away to roll into the dew covered grass. The sun is just lifting over the trees as he breaths his last breath and his blood waters the weeds by the railroad tracks.

Jack, who was a young man and before he had set out to travel the land, he'd been a bit fuller through the body. For all its shortcomings, at home there had been plenty of good food. He was still muscled it was true, but they were now the lean tendons created by lots of hard work and never enough food.

He was also strong; he had to be to make his way as he had for the last year or so. He could jump on the train with ease. He knew he could hold the frame with a sure hand and ride the underbelly for many miles before a railroad bull caught him at some stop. The danger was that he would grow tired, lulled by the endless rattle of the train along the steel, and lose his grip as muscles finally gave out.

Yet, he had always made it before and so he hustled along the train as it slowed for the grade and pulled himself on. This time, however, his luck ran out.

Losing his grip he fell to the ground and the hard rush of air, a low hanging piece of metal spun him around like a top. He was knocked unconscious in a split second, and never woke as the huge metal wheels carried tons of weight across his body, crushing his limbs, and scattering his mangled body along the line in a long bloody trail.

Pete who had hoisted himself on to the train and climbed to the catwalk atop the cars. He braced himself there, swaying as the car rolled over the land. He'd been stealing a ride for months now, jumping on and off where the train had to slow down to make a curve. It was near the road that led to the farm and easy enough to do.

The train slowed down as it headed into a series of gentle curves, his signal to climb down and get ready to jump off. It would have worked if the embankment hadn't given away during a short rain burst that totally reconfigured the slope of the land. Instead of jumping off to roll away from the heavy wheels, it now sloped steeply back, and was damp enough to rob him of any purchase. Instead of a safe landing, it spit him right back against the huge wheels as they grasped the steel of the rails.

Franklin who kept his eyes on the road and his ears open for the sound of the train. The job was getting a little too dicey lately with the railroad detectives, the Marshalls, and the local police poking their noses around. Of course, he'd told Ferguson that he was too quick to kill witnesses. When hardly anybody but a few stray sodbusters had lived out here it was easy to toss the goods off the train as it passed, hustle it aboard a mule and hurry to sell the whiskey, the guns, or whatever it might be that day.

It was one thing to rough up some rail crew too dirt poor to risk losing their jobs, or muscle some wet behind the years kids but lately, well there had been a couple of the guys a little too quick to pull a knife and slit a throat or clobber someone with a killing blow. Then it was bury them, toss them off a trestle, or drag their bodies on the track as t he 2 am to the City was expected. What with the telegraph, the telephone, and towns busting out like weeds, it was hard to feel safe anymore and he was getting too old. This was a young man's job that was for sure.

He rode the car, swaying slightly as he clutched the door-jamb, looking out the open door at the fields and pastures as they passed. At his feet were the bodies of the two young men who had been in the car when he climbed aboard and they had offered him food, a smoke, and even some water.

Shiftless, lazy louts, they all were anymore. They should be at home helping their parents on farms or tending some business. As the train made a slight curve, he kicked the two bodies out and knew that the chances were good it would be assumed they had been hit and killed by a train. Trains were such dangerous things, after all.

If he had sons to help him, well maybe the bankers and the railroad men would not have robbed him of his place. Then maybe his wife would have stayed as well.

He hated banks and railroads and that was strange seeing they were responsible for the skills he now used so well. He had become hired muscle to scare off rival companies, farmers, and anyone else they men with the money wanted to be someplace else. He had learned that he might have been a lousy farmer but he did some things well. He also learned he had a taste, maybe even a gift, for the work as well.

Beatings soon became murders and he as he honed his skill he learned some deaths the authorities just did not investigate too closely.

It was easy, he soon learned, to make some deaths look a lot like accidents. If a man was good at his work, and he was, why he might even get away with murder.

HEAR THAT LONESOME WHISTLE...

Standing on the rails in a small community, alongside a rusty, desolate and forgotten stretch of track, the wind seems to carry the haunting sounds of long ago. A person standing in that spot need only tilt the head to sense the echo of the chug of the steam, hear the long whistle, and feel the rattle and hum of the approaching train flow past.

As the train moves on down the track of Oklahoma history, some answers have been found to the causes of the numerous deaths reported along early rail lines. Evidence has shown that some were considered criminal at the time.

Enough questions remain about others, however, to suggest that perhaps one or more persons *unknown* used the railroad as a means of disposing of a body.

That person, or persons, used the dangerous rail lines to easily transit from one location to another, and maybe, just maybe, stop off occasionally to fulfill some darkly evil hunger in his soul.

When Death Rode the Rails

About the Author

Marilyn A. Hudson holds a B.A. in History and a Master's in Library and Information Studies. She has long been fascinated by the more unusual aspects of the past. In the process of researching for another project, intriguing articles of gory death kept catching her eye and the deeper she read the more interest turned to curiosity.

Her novel question about an early day serial killer has captured the attention and feedback of several members of law enforcement. Her work on the blog, "*Mystorical*," led to unearthing some fascinating tales of early Oklahoma often overlooked by traditional historians and city boosters. The result was *When Death Rode The Rails*.

Hudson is a member of the Organization of American Historians and has been a contributing editor and newspaper stringer. She is also author of "Elephant Hips Are Expensive", "One Night Club and a Mule Barn", "Off the Page: Basic Tips for Conducting a Story Time", "Annie Oklahoma", "Tales of Hell's Half Acre", and "The Bones of Summer."

"*Whether one believes a killer was at work, or merely enjoys history and the railroads*," notes the author, "'*When Death Rode the Rails*" *offers a glimpse at a different aspect of a forgotten corner of history.*"

WHORL BOOKS

If you enjoyed this 'Haunted by History', try these –

Whorl Books, Longer works:

Hudson, Marilyn A. **The Bones of Summer: Short Chilling Stories**

Hudson, Marilyn **A. Tales of Hell's Half Acre: Murder, Mayhem, and Mysteries in Early Oklahoma City.**

Hudson, Marilyn A. **When Death Rode the Rails: Strange Deaths Along Early Oklahoma Lines.**

Whorl Books, Forthcoming Titles:

Hudson, Cullan and Marilyn A. Hudson. **The Mound: a novel.**
A full length paranormal thriller set in modern day Oklahoma. Something is stirring in a historic old hotel…

Hudson, Marilyn A. **Foul Harvest**.
A full length novel about a serial killer driven to kill and a victim driven to survive.

whorlbooks@gmail.com
www.whorlbooks.blogspot.com

END NOTES

[1] "The Railroad Death Rate." Statistics of Vitality. Catskill Archive located at http://catskillarchive.com/rrextra/wkbkch22.html [accessed on 5/3/08].

[2] Federal Railroad Office of Safety Analysis Statistics – Homepage – at http://safetydata.fra.dot.gov/OfficeofSafety/; Bureau of Transportation Statistics at http://www.bts.gov/publications/national_transportation_statistics/2002/html/table_02_01.html

[3] Savage, Ian. "Trespassing on the Railroad." Research in Transportation Economics: Railroad Economics. Elsevier Science, 2007, 3.

[5] "Made a Gruesome Find". City in Brief. The Oklahoman (Jan. 29, 1902): 3.

[6] "General Curfew law" The Oklahoman (April 20, 1902): pg. 9.

"Homicide Rate Trends." Bureau of Justice Statistics located at http://www.ojp.usdoj.usdoj.gov/bjs/glance/tables/hmrttab.html [accessed on 5/3/2008].

[8] *Oklahoman* (Aug. 17, 1907: 10)

[9] Dale, Edward Everett and Morris L. Waddell. History of Oklahoma. (New York: Prentice-Hall, 1948): pg. 434.

[10] "Big Extensions" The Oklahoman (Jan. 25, 1902): pg. 5.

[11] "Railroad News: The Santa Fe Talking of Running A Line from Woodward to Quanah" The Oklahoman (April 16, 1902): pg.8.

[12] Dale, Edward Everett and Jesse Lee Rader. *Readings in Oklahoma History*. (Evanston, IL: Row, Peterson and Company, 1930); pg. 798.

[13] Dale, Edward Everett and Morris L. Waddell. *History of Oklahoma*. (New York: Prentice-Hall, 1948): pg. 431-435.

[14] *The Oklahoman* (May1, 1906): 2.

[15] "Scarcity of Men for Railroad Labor ." The Oklahoman (Nov. 25, 1908): pg. 9.
[16] Sarchet, C.M. "Railroad Camps Often Have Queer Mascots" The Oklahoman (Jul 26, 1914): pg. 5.

[17] "Modern Lucretia Borgia on Trial", The Oklahoman (Mar. 7, 1912):pg. 1.
[18] Ruth, pg 157, 208.
[19] Oklahoma Place names pg.95; Ruth, pg. 50,68, 90.

[20] "Mystery is Unsolved". The Oklahoman (March 30, 1906):1.

[21] "Apparently He Was Murdered." New York Times (February 21, 194):pg. 8 ; accessed at http://query.nytimes.com/mem/archive-free/pdf?_r=1&res=9A01EEDB1F39E033A25752C2A9649C94659ED7CE

22 Skeleton of an infant about 4 months old found in ditch along MKT tracks near the driving park." Waco, Texas (April 14, 1896): n.p.;"Walter Harper, KATY Brakeman, run over by Train". Ibid (July 27, 1896): n.p.; "Unknown Man Found Dead Aransas Pass railroad." August 22; 1898; "Sidney J. Evans run over by railroad car and dies". Ibid. March 16; "Walter Wester dies of injuries from railroad accident". Oct. 1, 1898; "W.P. Montgomery hit by Freight Train." May 15; "Bob Slaughter, age 17, was killed by railway train yesterday. Knocked off 1st street bridge." June 18; "Byron Kingsbury and "Dunk" Mclennon found dead with throats cut." Aug. 4;"Henry Thomas was killed yesterday under the wheels of the Buffalo Bill train near Hewitt. No family." Oct. 19; "Jack Standley killed by train 5 miles west of Waco". Sitting on tracks, a 45-year-old male thought to have been asleep. n/d; "Body Cut To Pieces," The Dallas News, dateline Woodbine, TX. (Oct. 29, 1900) at

(http://www.texasescapes.com/FallingBehind/ObituariesStruckOnTheHeadByLocomotive122703.htm)
[23] (http://www3.gendisasters.com/texas/4325/woodbine,-tx-train-accident,-oct-1900).

[24] Ibid. "C.M. Lewis, Pullman sleeping car conductor, found dead by railroad tracks, two miles west of Waco. Bullet hole in left temple." June 16, 1901; "D.A. Harris died suddenly near the KATY depot Saturday. Age 55. No known relatives." N.d. at (http://www.texasescapes.com/FallingBehind/ObituariesStruckOnTheHeadByLocomotive122703.htm)

[25] "Mystery": Man found dead near Anadarko August 26th Identified." The Oklahoman (Oct. 12, 1901): pg.1

[26] "Body Mutilated: German Baker Ground to Pieces by Railway Train at Wellston" The Oklahoman (Nov. 5, 1901):pg.1.

[27] "Beaten to Death with A Heavy Club": Almost Nude Body of a Man Found Near Shawnee…." The Oklahoman (Nov. 29, 1901) :pg. 1.

[28] "Foul Murder at Wagoner: A Man Found Dead In Heart of Town with Throat Cut". The Oklahoman (April 3, 1902): pg. 1.

[29] "His Head Crushed: And Awful Marks of Violence All Over His Person." The Oklahoman (August 5, 1902):pg. 1.

[30] "NO TITLE". Oct. 26, 1902; "Santa Fe Sued" The Oklahoman (March 30, 1904): pg. 3.

[31] "Coming to See New Line." The Oklahoman (Nov. 13, 1903):2.

[32] 'Choctaw, Oklahoma & Gulf R.R. Co. Time Table, in Effect June 21st, 1903." The Oklahoman (June 28, 1903):18.

[33] "Oklahoma Railroads." Oklahoman (Dec. 2, 1903): 1.

[34] "Help Wanted Male", Oklahoman (September 24, 1903), pg. 7.

[35] "Injured by a Train: Oklahoma City Boy Badly Mangled At Edmond: Supposed to have been riding under the Trucks…" The Oklahoman (July 26, 1903): 9.

[36] "Throat Was Cut", and the body dragged to a railroad track to hide the crime; Murder at Shawnee." The Oklahoman (Dec. 17, 1903).

[37] "Much Building", Oklahoman (April 27, 1904), pg. 7.
[38] "An Unknown Man, found Dead on the Choctaw Track East of City Yesterday". The Oklahoman (Jan. 29, 1904): pg. 26.

[39] "Murdered Man is Identified". The Oklahoman. (March 29, 1904): pg. 2.

[40] "Santa Fe Sued" The Oklahoman (March 30, 1904) : pg. 3.

[41] "Body of Boy is Identified: His Mother Had Supposed He Had Gone Away With A Rail Road Wrecking Crew." The Oklahoman. (April 14, 1904): pg. 3

[42] "Eason is Dead: Railroad Switchman injured in Frisco Yard Died Last Night." The Oklahoman (April 16, 1904): 7.

[43] "Body Was Found Near Frederick: Remains of a Man who had evidently been Murdered some time ago." The Oklahoman (April 24, 1904): pg. 4.

[44] "Struck By Train": Two Rock Island Officers Instantly Killed Sunday Night". The Oklahoman. (Nov. 8, 1904): 1.

[45] "Gruesome Find: A Farmer Near Jones City Found a Skull in His Dooryard: Whole Body Found Later." The Oklahoman (Dec. 18, 1904): pg. 3.

[46] "Trying to Locate a Missing Girl: Young Girl Who Disappeared Last Week From Fletcher Has Not Been Found" The Oklahoman (Dec. 23, 1904): 3.

[47] "Body Found in the Canadian: Remains of W.R. Dunn, Who Had Disappeared in November Fished Out." The Oklahoman. (Dec.30, 1904) pg.1 .

[48] "Froze to Death In Sight of Shelter" The Body of a Young Man Found Near The Railway Station at Coretta. "The Oklahoman. (Jan,. 11, 1905): pg. 1.

[49] "Double Murder Still a Mystery." The Oklahoman (Feb.1, 1905):pg. 1.

[50] "Railroad Man Badly Beaten: Head was pounded into a jelly by midnight assailant." The Oklahoman. (March 4, 1905):pg.1.

[51] "Skeleton Found in Tree", The Oklahoman, May 6 1905, Eufaula.

[52] "A Narrow Escape: Mother and Three Children Came Near Being Killed." The Oklahoman (June 1, 1905): pg. 2.

[53] "A Queer Story: railroad Laborer said fellow workman was shot by a policeman; Report caused Excitement." The Oklahoman. (June 14, 1905): pg. 7.

[54] "Murder Tahlequah", Oklahoman, June 21.
[55] "Ground to Pieces: Mangled Remains of Switchman Found On Rock Island Tracks Sunday", The Oklahoman (Sept. 26, 1905): pg. 3

[56] "Murder Charge Is Lodged Against Former Deputy Marshall at Ralston." The Oklahoman. (Nov. 2,1 905):pg. 2.

[57] *"Man beaten to death by tracks", Oklahoma, Nov. 11, 1905.*

[58] "May Be Murder: It is thought that the man Found Near the River Sunday is Not a Suicide." The Oklahoman. (Jan 12., 1906): pg. 5.

[59] Oral story collected, October 28, 2009, Oklahoma City.

[60] "Young Man's Head Ground to a Pulp: Finding of Body on Railroad track at Tulsa indicates Murder." The Oklahoman (April 24, 1906): pg. 6.

[61] "Lifeless Body of Young Man: Crushed between a flat car and pile of logs in local Santa Fe Yards." The Oklahoman., (Jun, 16, 1906): pg. 5.

[62] "Headless Body Found." Oklahoman, (July 28, 1906), pg. 12.

[63] "Boy's Mangled Body Found in Car of Wheat." Evening News, Ada, Oklahoma (July 9, 1906).

[64] "Boy's Mangled Corpse Found in Freight Care Where He Was Murdered By Tramp." Indiana Evening Gazette, Indiana, Pennsylvania (July 10, 1906).

[65] **"Horrible Find: Body of Young Priester of Tulsa Found in a Wheat Car near Tulsa."** The Oklahoman, (July 10, 1906): pg.1.

[66] "Find Murderers: Two Negroes Are Jailed for Killing Young Priester at Tulsa: Negro Jackson Confesses: Most Brutal in the History of the Indian Country – Body Horribly Mangled." The Oklahoman, (Aug. 5, 1906): pg. 12.

[67] "Three Killed: were asleep on the Frisco Railroad Tracks Near Bristow". The Oklahoman (July 29, 1906): pg. 4.

[68] "Drowned as He Was Drinking: Member of Frisco Section Gang Drowns While Body Is On Land." The Oklahoman. (Aug 2, 1906): pg. 3.

[69] "An Awful Death: Little Boy Ground Under the Wheels of a Rock Island Train: Body Not Yet Identified." The Oklahoman. (Aug. 10, 1906): 7.

[70] "Believe Iowan Was Robbed and Killed: Clothing of Missing Man Found Near Lawton, Basis of Suspicion." The Oklahoman (Oct. 19, 1906): pg. 1.

[71] "Reward of $2,000 Offered for Amarillo Murder," Oklahoma, (10/27/1906) pg 3.

[72] "Murdered Boy At Amarillo Earl Dockery of Oklahoman" , Oklahoman, (10/20/1906) pg. 2.

[73] "Mysterious Death Occurs at Harrah: Rock Island Employee Dies Suddenly After Prolonged Carousal." The Oklahoman (Jan.1, 1907) :pg. 5.

[74] "Switchman Tries to Cut Enemy's Throat: After Fist Fight He Wielded Razor in Chickasha Restaurant". The Oklahoman (Jan. 24, 1907) : pg. 11.

[75] "Body Found Not that of Meadows: Identification Held Not Sure", Oklahoman (July 12, 1907),pg. 1; "Jury Hears the Story of the Passion." Oklahoman (July 8, 1908): pg. 1.; "Is Meadows Still Living?", Oklahoman (Sept.8, 1910), pg. 1. See *Tales of Hell's Half Acre* by Marilyn A. Hudson for further discussion of this case.

[76] "Skull is Found." Oklahoman (June 26, 1907),pg. 2.

[77] "Practical Jokers placed skull by a country road." Oklahoman, (July 14, 1907), pg. 4.

[78] "Form Association to Probe Murder": Tulsa Citizens Still Determined to Solve Mystery of Priester Case." The Oklahoman (Jan 26, 1907): pg. 4.

[79] "Mangled On Tracks: Fragmentary Remains of Young Man Found by Frisco Engine Crew." The Oklahoman (Feb. 21, 1907): pg.1.

[80] "Body Mangled on the Track: Jack Du Bois Run Down and Killed by Santa Fe Train". The Oklahoman. (Feb. 26, 1907): pg. 7.

[81] "Jack Dubois Choked A Boy." The Oklahoman. (Dec. 24, 1904):pg. 5.

[82] "Held for murdering a farmer near Dewy." Oklahoman, 2/26.

[83] "Put Body in Track To Hide Their Crime: Henryetta Man is Shot To Death: Trainman Not Responsible." The Oklahoman (Feb. 28, 1907): pg. 3.

[84] "Oklahoma Man Slain in Iowa?: Body Found in Car Believed that of Bert Madden." The Oklahoman (March 20, 1907): pg. 3.

[85] "Sleeps on Track; Struck By Train." The Oklahoman (April 20, 1907): pg9

[86] "Parents Searching for Missing Boy" The Oklahoman (May 3, 1907):pg. 7.

[87] "Grewsome [sic] Find is made in Car: Body of Lad, Crushed to Death, Discovered in Chickasha". The Oklahoman (June 5, 1907): pg. 8.

[88] "Mystery Attaches to Death of Brakeman on Freight: Skull Shows Fracture; Questions of Whether Man was Murdered is Being Investigated." The Oklahoman (June 29, 1907): 1.

[89] "Mystery Attaches to death of a brakeman; Skull shows fracture". Oklahoman June29, Norman, pg.2

[90] "Corpse in River Food for Fishes": Ghastly Find By A Red River Ferryman Near Yarnby" (The Oklahoman (July 17,1907): 12.

[91] "Dead Man's Gulch", Oklahoman, July 26-28, 1907
"Lawton Police Arrest Quintette for Box Car Murder. Killing Was Near Here. Rock Island Brakeman from Shawnee who found Body is Held." The Oklahoman. (July 30, 1907): pg. 1.

[92] "Who is the dead man with ears gone?" The Oklahoman, Aug 3, 1907 pg. 4.; "On A Hot Scent, Detectives Say: Arrests in Gunreth Murder Case Are Expected Within A Week." The Oklahoman (August 9, 1907):pg. 12; "Doesn't Identify Murder Suspects" The Oklahoman (Sept. 11, 1907):pg9; "Gunreth Killed Because He Assaulted Small Girl?" The Oklahoman (Aug. 7, 1907):pg. 5; "Governor Fails to Tell Sheriff" The Oklahoman (Aug. 14, 1907):pg. 4.

[93] "Ranchman mangled body found on tracks" Aug 7, 1907, pg. 7

[94] "Murdered Man's Body Discovered: Aged Negro His Head Gashed, Is Found in Coal Pit." The Oklahoman (Aug. 14, 1907):pg. 6.

[95] "20 year old trestle, Shawnee, Aug 21, 1907

[96] "Neck Broken by a 20-Foot Fall." The Oklahoman. (Sept. 12, 1907): 1.

[97] "Dogs pick bones of corpse at Frederick" Sept. 30/Oct. 1 pg. 4

[98] "Probe Indicates Murder At Enid: Coroner's Jury Believed Body was Put on Track to Hide Crime." The Oklahoman (Oct. 5, 1907): pg.1.

[99] Canadian victim, Shawnee, December. Uncited newspaper clipping, private collection.

[100] "Coal Heaver's Death Mystifies Officers" The Oklahoman (Dec. 18) 1907): pg.8.

[101] "Negro Killed Under a Train: Body is Horribly Mangled, Believed To Have Been Stealing A Ride." The Oklahoman (Jan. 2, 1908) pg. 8.

[102] "Headless Boyd of A Missing Farmer Found Near River": believed to be John Sparks who Disappeared A Year Ago." The Oklahoman (March 15, 1908): pg.1.

[103] "Dynamite and Evidences of Murder Found: Gruesome Find of Blood-Bespattered Mattress Near Railroad Track." The Oklahoman. (April 1, 1908):pg. 6.

[104] "Victim of a Foul Murder: Man with Skull Crushed Picked up Near Railroad Is Dead." The Oklahoman (April 8, 1908): pg. 5.

[105] "Not Sure that it is Murder". The Oklahoman. (June 12, 1908);pg. 3.

[106] "Two Held Charged with Murder of a Red Man At Nowata." The Oklahoman (Aug. 19, 1908): pg. 7.

[107] "Mystery's Veil Drawn About Stranger's Death: Dead Body Discovered Near Heart of City Soon After Dusk: Murder or Accident? Corpse found on Railroad Bears Strange Woods and No Clue to Identity." The Oklahoman (Dec. 17, 1908) : pg.1.

[108] "Tulsa Man Has Throat Cut". The Oklahoman (Dec. 19, 1908): pg. 10.

[109] "Fail to Identify Railroad Victim: Coroner's Jury Says Cars Killed Man in the Santa Fe Yard." The Oklahoman (Dec. 20, 1908): pg 19.

[110] "Hold Inquest Today Over Body Found Near Deep Fork". The Oklahoman (Dec. 29, 1908):pg.5.

[111] **"Body Beside Track Indicates A Murder: Unknown Man Found with Throat Cut-Body Taken To Tulsa." The Oklahoman. (Jan.2, 1909): pg. 5.**

[112] **"Staring Corpse of Six Months Yet Unclaimed: Body Found in Katy Yards At Muskogee in the Morgue." The Oklahoman (Jan.15, 1909): pg. 1.

[113] "Boy is Bound and Gagged for 28 Hours." The Oklahoman (Jan. 24, 1909): pg. 16.

[114] "Unknown Man Found With His Throat Cut" The Oklahoman. (March 9, 1909): pg. 7.

[115] "Goes Fishing: Found Headless By Track". The Oklahoman. (May 23, 1909):20.

[116] "Arrest Made in Case of Negro Found Dead on Frisco Tracks: Authorities Active: Capture Suspect while Permitting Self-Slaying Theory

to be Bruited." The Oklahoman. (Aug.3, 1909): 1: "New Move in Brooks Case" (The Oklahoman)pg. 1.

[117] "Ghastly Find on Railroad Track: fragments of Unknown Boy's Body Strewn For 600 Yards." The Oklahoman (August 29, 1909): pg. 7.

[118] "Meets Horrible Death Under the M.K. &T. Train" The Oklahoman Aug. 29, 1909): pg.9.

[119] "Emaciated Body of Man Found: Murder Suspected: Unknown Victim's Bones Lay in Thicket on Washita River." The Oklahoman (Sept. 14, 1909): pg.3.

[120] "Unknown Body of Man Found at Chickasha That of Synder" The Oklahoman (Sept. 28, 1909): pg. 3.

[121] "Body Thought to be That of Midland Valley Agent". The Oklahoman (Oct..6, 1909):n.p..

[122] **"His Throat Cut, Farmer of Sallisaw Will Die: J.B. Jones Found Half Mile from Home – Money Missing."** The Oklahoman (Oct. 26, 1909): 3.

[123] "Fight for Honor May End in Death: Sapulpa Woman's Throat Cut from ear to Ear by Unknown Fiend." The Oklahoman. (Nov. 17, 1909): 1.

[124] "Hack Driver Arrested for Muskogee Murder: Charles Blade of Aurora Mo Has head Severed by Car." The Oklahoman (Nov. 30, 1909) pg. 2.

[125] **"Gruesome Find in Box By Railroad Men."** The Oklahoman. (Jan 2, 1910): n.p.

[126] "Mystery Enshrouds Death of Oklahoma Student." The Oklahoman (Feb.27, 1910): pg. 21

[127] "Unknown Murder Victim is Buried: Body Found in Box Car 35 Months Ago Interred in Pauper's Grave." The Oklahoman. (May 2, 1910): pg. 3.

[128] Chickasha Has Fourth Mystery: Decomposed Body of Man with Hole in Skull Found". The Oklahoman. (Jun. 22, 1910):pg. 10.

[129] "Body of Unknown Found in River: Badly Decomposed Body of Stranger Ordered Buried." The Oklahoman. (Aug.23, 1910): pg. 12.

[130] "Mystery in Death of Red Fork Man: The Body of Marvin Bowly is found by the Railroad Tracks." The Oklahoman. (Nov. 29, 1910): pg. 3.

[131] "Frisco Absolved from All Blame: Coroner's Jury Holds That Killing of G.T. Gwinn Was Accidental" The Oklahoman. (Dec. 1, 1910): 5.

[132] "Body is Found in Railroad yards: Police of Davis Believe That Claud Johnson was Murdered." The Oklahoman (Jan. 9, 1911): pg. 6.

[133] "Identification from Toe Nail: Body of Boy Killed By Train at Tulsa Recognized by Brother." The Oklahoman. (Feb., 1, 1911): pg. 4.

[134] Husband Slain: Wife Attacked: Murderous Assailant Then Places Both Bodies on Track." The Oklahoman (July 28, 1911): pg. 11.

[135] "Murder Mystery Near M'Alester: Indian's Body Run Over By Train – Two Arrested. Bore Knife Wounds." The Oklahoma. (Nov. 5, 1911): pg. 15.

[136] "Ear-Snipped Body is Identified by Photo" The Oklahoman. (Dec. 19, 1911): pg. 1.

[137] "Lad Falls From Train; Is Killed: Body of Wichita Boy is Picked Up at Renfrow Depot." The Oklahoman. (Aug. 2, 1912): pg. 3

[138] "Jack the Ripper Still At Large: No Trace of Assailant Of Mrs. Ida Jones, Who Will Die." The Oklahoman (Aug. 15, 1912): pg. 5
[139] "Youth is Slain by Unknown Man". Oklahoman (February 26, 1912), pg. 26.

[140] Stopped on Track, Struck by Train: Three Boys On Way to School Are Probably Fatally Injured." The Oklahoman (May 15, 1913): pg. 4.

[141] "While Slumbering: Victims…Bodies Strewn in Bits Along the Track." The Oklahoman. (Sept. 10, 1913): 1.

[142] "Story of Kiefer Murder Related: Witness Tells of Finding Body of Little Girl in Horrible Condition." The Oklahoman. (Jan. 29, 1914): pg. 1.

[143] "Former Soldier Takes Own Life: Body Found Near Railroad Station at Chickasha; Love Troubles." The Oklahoman (March 25, 1914): pg. 3.

[144] "Body of Youth Unidentified: He Was Fatally Hurt on Interurban Near Needham Saturday". The Oklahoman (June 10, 1914): pg. 3.

[145] Personal Interview, Velma Terry, September 1995.

[146] "Unidentified Tramp's Body Discovered by Rock Island Section Crew." The Oklahoman (Oct. 29, 1914): pg. 8.

[147] Actually, the Iowa case was one of several instances of similar axe welding murders from, at least, Colorado to Missouri and from Iowa to Louisiana between 1909 and 1914. Earlier cases of a similar nature can be traced to California and West Virginia where entire families were killed (using guns and axes). In two cases fires were went in an attempt to cover the deed. Some have noted the proximity of railroads in several of these, but this will need further research to verify.

[148] "Mystery Shrouds Hatchet Murders." Oklahoman, (Nov. 1, 1914), pg. 15.

[149] Oklahoman, (June 13, 1915), pg. 16.

[150] "Victim's Body is Placed on Tracks: Telegraph Operator at Antlers Slugged and Office is Robbed." The Oklahoman (Sept. 17, 1915): pg. 3.

[151] "Muskogee Woman IS Charged With Murder." Oklahoman (Sept. 3, 1915): pg.1.

[152] Woman's Body is Still Unclaimed: Suicide Remains Mystery After Week of Search for Clue." The Oklahoman (May 31, 1917): 2.

[153] "Unidentified Man Kills Himself: Body, With Throat Cut, Is Found Near City: Had Refused to Tell Name." The Oklahoman. (Feb. 17, 1918): 10.

[154] "Boy Sues Road for $10,000 As Damages." The Oklahoman (Feb.20, 1918):16.

[155] "Body of Youth Unidentified: He was fatally Hurt on Interurban Near Needham." The Oklahoman (June 10, 1918): 3.

[156] "Narrow Escape For Boy Asleep on Railway Track." The Oklahoman (Aug.3, 1919): 37.

[157] "Train Kills Boy Asleep on Tracks: Companion Saved by Jump While Asleep." The Oklahoman (Sept. 18, 1919): 4.

[158] "Train Gang Worker is Found Murdered": D.E. Stinton Killed in a Box Car Near Henryetta." The Oklahoman. (Jan. 21, 1920): pg. 4.

[159] 'Mangled Body Is Found at Ardmore." The Oklahoman. (Sept. 15, 1920): 5.

[160] "Tripods and Vibration Dampening", Video help, http://www.videohelp.com/forum/archive/tripods-and-vibration-dampening-any-proven-suggestions-t366277.html

[161] "Coal Miner's Daughter" (1980).

[162] "UP: Steam Locomotives." UPRR, at http://www.uprr.com/aboutup/excurs/up844.shtml.

[163] "Land speed record for locomotives," Wikipedia, at http://en.wikipedia.org/wiki/Land_speed_record_for_rail_vehicles

[164] Harris, Miller, Miller, Hanson. "Basic Ground Borne Vibration Concepts" at http://www.hmmh.com/cmsdocuments/FTA_Ch_07.pdf

[165] "Decibel Loudness Comparison Chart," Galen Carol Audio, at http://www.gcaudio.com/resources/howtos/loudness.html

[166] "Noise and Hearing Loss." American Speech Language Association, at http://www.asha.org/public/hearing/disorders/noise.htm

[167] "Safety", http://nmgrip.com/upload/images/PDF/Noise%20&%20Safety%2010-30-07.pdf

[168] Piker, Suzie, "2 Teen Girls, Injured: Cope with Change," at National Public Radio http://www.npr.org/templates/story/story.php?storyId=100875845.

[169] "The Boss Who Fell Asleep On a Railroad Track", at London Evening Standard, http://www.thisislondon.co.uk/news/article-23378371-the-boss-who-fell-asleep-on-a-railway-track.do

[170] Boag, Peter .Same-Sex Affairs: *Constructing and Controlling Homosexuality in the Pacific Northwest. University of California, 1992. pg. 37.*

[171] Schechter, Harold. The Serial Killer Files, pg. 6-8.

[172] Norris, J. Serial killers: The growing Menace. New York: Doubleday, 1988.

[173] Harrington, Michael. "Victorian Psycho." National Review. (1/23/95):47:1.

[174] Forney, Matthew. "Predatory Transients." Time South Pacific (12/1/2003);p. 36.

[175] Several books, Serial Killers: The Methods and Madness of Monsters (Peter Vronksy), Encyclopedia of Unsolved Crimes (Michael Newton) and Still at Large: A Case book of 20th Century Serial Killers (Michael Nicotan) mention these Louisiana and Texas slayings.

Made in the USA
Charleston, SC
10 June 2013